G. STEWART MIDDLETON,
ARBROATH,
1977.

A PERSONAL ADVENTURE IN PROPHECY

RAYMOND McFARLAND KINCHELOE

A PERSONAL ADVENTURE IN PROPHECY

UNDERSTANDING
REVELATION

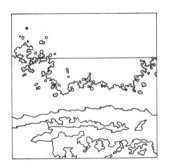

TYNDALE HOUSE PUBLISHERS WHEATON ILLINOIS
COVERDALE HOUSE PUBLISHERS LONDON ENGLAND

Library of Congress Catalog Card Number 74-80149
ISBN 8423-4815-8 cloth; 8423-4816-6 paper

Copyright © 1974 by Tyndale House Publishers, Inc.,
Wheaton, Illinois. All rights reserved.

First printing, June 1974

Printed in the United States of America

CONTENTS

FOREWORD

The Book of Revelation has traditionally been the most difficult part of the New Testament to interpret. Calvin declined to write a commentary on it, and Adam Clarke almost reached the same decision.

What we really need is a guide for our own study of the book. And that is exactly what the author has provided. He has carefully marked out a program which will lead any intelligent, sincere Christian into a better understanding of the Apocalypse.

Most books on Revelation are highly speculative. and propound a single—often narrow—point of view. The strength of this volume is that it forces the reader to make his own appraisal of what the Scripture actually says before he faces the interpretations of others.

It is a pleasure to commend this book to all who seek to know what God's Word says about the final outcome of history.

Ralph Earle, Professor of New Testament
Nazarene Theological Seminary
Kansas City, Missouri

PREFACE

Bible study has always fascinated me, but a new day dawned when I discovered that each of the sixty-six books could be approached in a methodical way; that under the guidance of the Holy Spirit we can find the actual viewpoint of the author; that this viewpoint reveals the author's basic pattern; and that the composition of the books of the Bible follows the same basic laws and yields to the same structural analyses as any other kind of writing.

Since then I have had a keen desire to share this discovery by demonstrating how to study any particular book of the Bible. I have chosen the most modern and perhaps most misunderstood of all the sixty-six books—The Revelation!

The purpose of this volume is to help intelligent readers discover basic principles that will enable them with the help of the Holy Spirit to unfold this glorious Revelation of Jesus Christ. I would also like to encourage every reader to form the habit of independent, inductive Bible study, so that he will be eager to investigate the other sixty-five books of God's precious Word.

This study is based on the premise that God's Word was written to be understood, and that each of its books has a message for us as well as its original readers. Although I do not claim infallibility in interpreting the Revelation, I do heartily recommend the methods of study presented in Chapters 1 and 4, and I urge the reader to consider thoughtfully the findings in the other chapters. One special request—please exhaust all the possibilities of your own independent study (as suggested at the beginning of each chapter) before reading the remainder of each chapter.

I make no apologies for assuming that the original manuscripts of the Bible are verbally inspired, that they are a complete revelation of God's will for the salvation of man, and that they constitute the only authoritative rule of Christian faith and practice. Since the Book of Revelation centers around Christ, I would also like to emphasize that Christ is not merely a historic Person who actually died on the cross, but that he is also God the Son, eternally alive with God the Father and God the Holy Spirit.

In this volume the Book of Revelation is treated from a premillenarian, modified-futuristic viewpoint. I do not subscribe to all the implications of dispensational teaching, but I do distinguish seven different methods of God's dealing with mankind, though without erecting barriers which prevent certain privileges and responsibilities of man from extending from one age to another. For example, the privileges and responsibilities of human government, which began in the days of Noah, will continue until the reign of Christ in the millennium. However, I have no intentions of forcing my views upon the unsuspecting reader. My main objective is to encourage the reader to become an independent investigator of truth. He should consider the findings of this volume as simply one of the several viewpoints of evangelicals today.

Although the King James Version of 1611 contains beautiful Elizabethan English and is the most familiar translation of the Bible to most readers, the American Standard Revised Version of 1901 has the advantage of manuscripts discovered since 1611, such as the Sinaitic, the Vatican, the Alexandrian, and the Ephraem. Scholars of the late nineteenth century had a better knowledge of Hebrew, Greek, and related languages than seventeenth-century translators, and they had the advantage of a more highly developed science of textual criticism. The grouping of verses into paragraphs is also a great improvement over the King James arrangement. For these reasons all references, unless otherwise indicated, are from the American Standard Revised Version.

I heartily wish to acknowledge the following sources of help in compiling this volume: Harold Meredith Freligh, Merrill C. Tenney, and Ralph Earle, my beloved professors; Joseph Augustus Seiss, Richard Charles Henry Lenski, William Newell, and Robert Traina, whose writings have been of special help; the students who have been in my classes over a period of twenty-three years—by their challenging questions and by their thoughtful contributions; and my beloved wife, Christina Rebekah, who has worked closely with me in revising the manuscript and making helpful suggestions.

—Raymond M. Kincheloe

PART ONE

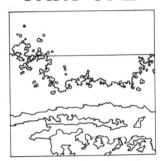

BASIC METHODS
OF BIBLE STUDY

1

GETTING READY FOR TODAY'S
GREATEST ADVENTURE

Certain basic principles of Bible study apply to every book of the Bible, and we will discuss some of these methods in this introductory chapter. If you have not already done so, please read the preface before proceeding any further. After this you will be ready to consider Alexander Graham Bell's rule for a lifelong process of self-education.

The education of the mind is, after all, not a mere question of remembering facts which someone else gives us. The mind should conduct its own education to a larger extent. And it cannot do this unless it thinks for itself. A mind that does not reason is comparatively useless.

I have given the subject of self-education a great deal of thought and have evolved what you might call a "Rule of Three" in regard to it. The rule is simply this: "Observe! Remember! Compare!"

First, observe concrete facts; then use the memory of these facts to compare them, and to note their likenesses and differences.

Think that over, and you will see that it is the way

3

in which all knowledge is gained. The successful businessman is the one who has observed, remembered, and compared the facts of business. All the achievements of science have come from doing these three things. The extent to which *anyone does* them will measure the extent of his education and of his ability to continue to educate himself.

The very first essential of any real education is to observe. Without that you have no material out of which to manufacture knowledge. Remember what you have observed. Compare the facts you have observed, and you will find yourself thinking out conclusions.

These conclusions are real knowledge, and they are your own.

That was what made John Burroughs a great naturalist, Morgan a great financier, Napoleon a great general. It is the foundation of all education. And the wonderful thing about it is that gaining an education in this way is not a penance, but a delight.[1]

Now read the rest of this chapter. Think through each suggestion and refer to the Scriptures which illustrate each principle of study. You may need to reread parts of this chapter several times in order to make these study methods your very own, but the effort will be well repaid, for studying the Revelation is today's greatest adventure.

THE PLAN FOR THE ADVENTURE

Did it ever occur to you that Bible study can be a thrilling adventure? A thought-trip through God's inspired Word is far more exciting than a million-dollar, round-the-world excursion! Starting at Genesis, you would soon discover that at the

---

[1]/Alexander Graham Bell, as quoted by Mary B. Mullett, "How to Keep Young Mentally," *The Reader's Digest*, (February, 1922), p. 5. Condensed from *The American Magazine*, copyright 1922, The Reader's Digest Association, Inc. Reprinted by permission.

very dawn of creation God himself created this whole universe without the use of pre-existing materials. You would see how he dramatically formed the first helpmate for man and got the human race off to an ideal start in an ideal world. Adam was the king of all living creatures, and Eve was his queen-assistant.

A marvelously unique being, man had been created with the power to choose. As the first man, Adam found himself in a world where he must choose to either please God or listen to Satan. In this either/or proposition, Eve was deceived but Adam sinned knowingly and voluntarily, choosing to disobey God's will. The period called *Innocence* crashed to an end when Satan effected the fall of man and God's first family was expelled from the Garden of Eden (Gen. 3:1-24).

Adam soon found out that the knowledge of good and evil did not bring with it the power to choose good. His special new faculty for perceiving moral distinctions came to be called *conscience,* but Adam and his descendants soon discovered that apart from God even conscience is not a safe guide. A few years later murder, polygamy, and mixed marriages resulted in the judgment of the flood (Gen. 6—8).

Then God gave man a new beginning. When Noah and his family walked out of the ark, their new responsibility of *human government* (Gen. 9:6) was an advance over the previous arrangement. Man was now to govern the world for God. This new arrangement still exists, and will continue until Christ himself reigns during the Millennium (Rev. 20). But Noah soon failed under his plan, and his intoxication resulted in the sin of Ham and ultimately the curse of Canaan (Gen. 9:20-27).

Would God now destroy this generation of people by another flood? No, he chose to work through another family, calling out Abram (Gen. 12) and teaching him separation from the other peoples of the world. Abram was then given the *promise* of a son, and his name was changed to Abraham, meaning "the father of a multitude." Abraham was to be the father of the faithful, and through him the Messiah would come (Gal. 3:16). But Abraham failed by trying to bring the promised heir into the world by the works of the flesh. The result was the birth of Ishmael, the progenitor of the Arabs, who are still prominent in world history today. But in spite of the failure God gave to Abraham Isaac, the true heir.

Since the world was not yet ready for the birth of Christ, God used the *Law* (Exod. 20) to show man his sinful condition and to make him conscious of his great need of a Savior. The test of this era between Moses and Christ was obedience to the Mosaic Covenant, but there was failure even before Moses came down from the mountain. He found his people worshipping a calf of gold and practicing nudism (Exod. 32). These Israelites later failed to enter the Promised Land, failed under the judges, failed under the kings, and failed under the prophets. Then Christ came.

Soon after this the period of the *Law* ended in the great judgment of the sins of the world—the judgment upon the spotless Lamb of God (Jn. 1:29). The timeless Cross (Rev. 13:8, KJV) became an actual event in the history of the world—an event so important that the calendars of the world are reckoned before and after Christ. Calvary ushered in the New Covenant of *Grace,* an age which (along with human government) continues to the present.

The present church age of grace offers man the greatest advantages he has ever known. The sin question has been settled, and the grace of God is offered to the chiefest of sinners. Being justified by faith, we have peace with God, and his righteousness is imputed to all who come to Christ (Rom. 4: 22, 24). Moreover, by the regenerating power of the Holy Spirit the very righteousness of Christ is imparted to the believer (Tit. 3:5). However, in spite of the blessings of justification, regeneration, and sanctification, both Jews and Gentiles are failing to appropriate these manifestations of grace, and the church is not adequately reaching the nations of the world with the blessed news of redemption. Today iniquity is abounding, apostasy is widespread, and a large percentage of Christendom is shallow, ineffective, and lukewarm. It will take the woes of the Great Tribulation to awaken some to their great need for Christ-centered living. Others will be hardened by these same judgments rather than converted. Man has failed in every age so far.

The Revelation of Jesus Christ shows how this age of

grace will close with the judgment of the Great Tribulation and how Christ will return personally and visibly to reign for one thousand years (Rev. 20). Though the *Millennium* will be an age of peace, longevity, and righteousness, man will once again fail (Rev. 20:7-9). He failed in his ideal beginning in *innocence;* his *conscience* proved to be a poor guide; he failed in every form of *human government;* he failed to believe God's *promise* of a Savior; he did not keep God's *Law;* he is spurning this present day of *grace;* and if he is not careful, he will be deceived by Satan at the end of the *Millennium!*

THE PURPOSE OF THE ADVENTURE

A thorough study of the Revelation will not only prepare the child of God for the present *conflict* in the church but will make the *hope* of the church come alive to him! One backslidden college professor was restored to a vital faith in Christ solely through studying the Revelation. Social science had been his college major, but the Second World War shattered all his hopes of improvement in the world. After studying the Book of Revelation, however, he found meaning and purpose in the present by seeing the heavenly viewpoint of the future.

All that was lost to the human race in Genesis is regained in Revelation. In Genesis we find a curse and in Revelation we see a new creation. Genesis begins the story of redemption and Revelation climaxes the thrilling saga. In Genesis Satan enters and in Revelation he makes his exit. In Genesis the tree of life is lost but in Revelation the same tree is regained. In Genesis there is separation and isolation but in Revelation there is reunion and communion. In Genesis fellowship is lost but in Revelation fellowship is restored. In Genesis Paradise is lost but in Revelation Paradise is regained. In every way Revelation is the consummation of the revealed Word of God!

In these days of drastic change in world attitudes, alert people are sincerely wondering what attitudes and actions they as individuals should adopt. Are they justified in retreating into the security of isolationism and indifference, or should they cry aloud for a reviving invasion of the Holy Spirit into their lives? "Could it be," they ask "that we will witness the second coming of our Lord? Could he come any day now? Is Satan now bursting into his last struggle? Are we to fear him? Is it high time for the second coming of Jesus to become a purifying hope in our lives?" Today the person who is searching for answers to these questions will study the Revelation, and to him the book will unfold. It is the only book in the New Testament that is completely devoted to prophecy, and it is the only book in the New Testament that was written because of a direct command of the Lord. The Revelation is the most modern book in existence, for its events could begin at any time!

THE PREPARATION FOR THE ADVENTURE

Physical Preparation

Since the study method which we recommend is based on paragraphs rather than individual verses, we suggest that you obtain a copy of *The American Standard Version of the Bible* (1901). Though it is often worthwhile to read various Bible translations, we recommend that you avoid commentaries and Bible study notes until you have first studied the Scriptures themselves. Never let anybody's commentary be your center of gravity; give God a chance to speak first! Always strive for an immediate, firsthand experience in his Word.

Your next step should be to provide a good study environment, including adequate lighting in a quiet, uninterrupted location. Be sure to provide proper study aids, such as paper, pencil, pen, study table, and a comfortable chair. The goal is a keen mind in a relaxed body. Usually this is not possible after a heavy meal. Matthew Henry is said to have written his monumental commentary between the hours of four and eight in the morning, when his mind was freshest.

Spiritual Preparation

The spirit of prayer

Even more important than any of the foregoing is your spiritual preparation. The first step in spiritual preparedness is prayer. The Word of God is a living book, and it must be approached reverently and prayerfully. Horace Bushnell once said, "My experience is that the Bible is dull when I am dull. When I am really alive, and set upon the text with a tidal pressure of living affinities, it opens and multiplies discoveries, revealing depths even faster than I can note them." Let prayer, then, be your first approach to Bible study.

The spirit of truth
The second step in spiritual preparation is to recognize your utter dependence on the Holy Spirit to illumine your mind to what has already been recorded by divine inspiration. Christ said, "When he, the Spirit of truth, is come, he shall guide you into all the truth; for he shall not speak from himself, but what things soever he shall hear, these shall he speak; and he shall declare unto you the things that are to come" (John 16:13).

The spirit of obedience
The third step is to obey what God shows you in the Word. Bible study is a moral issue. To see truth without applying it to your life is fatal. Light rejected becomes darkness, and how great is that darkness! "But if we walk in the light, as he is in the light, we have fellowship one with another, and the blood of Jesus his Son cleanseth us from all sin" (1 John 1:7). The cleansed heart is the receptive heart. "The natural man receiveth not the things of the Spirit of God, for they are foolishness unto him and he cannot know them, because they are spiritually judged" (1 Cor. 2:14). On the other hand, God promises to unfold his Word to those who are walking with him (1 Cor. 2:10).

Mental Preparation

The author's basic pattern
Even though the Bible is the inspired Word of God, it was written for the human mind and by human beings who thought, acted, and lived in much the same way as the modern reader, though in a somewhat different environment. But truth has not changed; it remains the same. For this reason we can expect to find that the writings of Scripture harmonize with the basic laws of rhetoric, and, since they are inspired, that they are the greatest works of literature in all the world.

We can expect to find in any given book of the Bible a basic pattern into which the author has molded his content. For example, instead of reading Revelation indiscriminately, like a sponge, and thus being confused by the vast amount of detail, we should look for key phrases such as "after these things" and "I was in the Spirit." We should also attempt to find the specific relations in which the data are presented. John Ruskin said, "A musician composes an air by putting notes together in certain relations; a poet composes a poem by putting thoughts and words in pleasant order." In the same way an author conveys his thoughts to his readers by putting his ideas and suggestions in an appropriate order. We can find a remarkably definite order in studying the Revelation, and once we discover this arrangement the Revelation unfolds before our eyes more clearly than a television program!

Sometimes the form is indicated in a key verse, as in the Gospel of Mark: "For the Son of man also came (Preparation, Mark 1:1-13) not to be ministered unto, but to minister (Proclamation, Mark 1:14—10:52), and to give his life a ransom for many" (Passion, Mark 11:1—16:20).

Or the form might be indicated by the repetition of identical or similar key expressions, such as "from that time" in Matthew (4:17; 16:21). The Book of Revelation also contains key verses and significant expressions which indicate the pattern of the author. These help us discover sections and subsections for a possible charting of the book.

The author's point of view

It is also important for us to determine the author's point of view. The words of any book or document are the result of selection and emphasis. So the reader should discover *how* and *why* the author has arranged or elaborated his treatment. Few books of the Bible contain any preface which discloses the author's viewpoint, but every book contains certain cues to its structural relation and framework.

The first cue is *biographical.* Here the author may indicate his point of view by emphasizing a particular person or the interrelation of different personalities to each other. This is especially true in Genesis, where Cain is contrasted with

Abel, Abraham with Lot, Jacob with Esau, and Joseph with his brothers.

The second cue is *geographical,* and in this case *locality* is the significant feature. The Book of Exodus is a good example of this viewpoint.

The third cue is *historical,* with the emphasis on *events.* The Book of Numbers, with all the journeys and wanderings of Israel, illustrates this viewpoint.

The fourth cue is *chronological.* Here the *time element* is prominent, as in the Gospel of John, where certain feasts are used to date the events.

The fifth cue is *logical or ideological.* Here the structure depends on the elaboration of an idea or the succession of ideas within a passage, as in Romans. These viewpoints are not mutually exclusive, for John's Gospel fits into both the fourth and fifth classifications. These correspond somewhat to the questions of a reporter: Who? Where? What? When? Why? How?

We recommend that you first read the entire Book of Revelation at one sitting, in order to get a bird's-eye view of the whole book and to find the author's basic structural arrangement. The book may open to you at the very first reading or it may require several readings, each based on a different reading cue. By persisting in various methods of approach the book will soon begin to unfold, and you will have the joy of a firsthand encounter with the Word!

The author's structural units

After determining the basic pattern or form of Revelation, decide on a tentative name for each of its main divisions. As you first survey the book, look for an appropriate title, the key verse or verses, the key word or words, the identification of the author and his purpose, and the names and characteristics of the recipients.

Then begin a detailed study of the paragraphs, segments, sections, and divisions of the book. In some editions of the Bible the paragraphs will be obvious, but in certain passages you may disagree with the editors. When this happens, combine or divide paragraphs as the subject matter may dictate. In certain brief books like Philemon, you may wish to make each verse a separate paragraph.

A *segment* is a group of paragraphs, and this term is really synonymous with "chapter." But *your* segment may not coincide with the regular chapter divisions in your Bible! Make your own segments by combining these paragraphs which incorporate a single subject or phase of the book.

Then combine your segments into *sections,* and group these sections into *divisions.* (Or you might wish to include "subsections" between "segments" and "sections." See page 30 for instructions on making a paragraph chart with diagonal lines.) The names you choose may be descriptive, analytical, or interpretive. A good way to get started is to isolate a key word or two from the paragraph, leaving the interpretation of the whole until later. At this point in the observing process avoid both interpretation and application, concentrating only only on what you actually see in the text.

The author's structural relations

How can you be sure you have really found the author's pattern, and that you have not imposed your own concepts on the book? First, pay special attention to structural relations between paragraphs, segments, sections, and divisions. Here are some of the laws of relationship.

Comparison or contrast. The laws of comparison or contrast show the association of like or opposite things, as illustrated in the seven churches of Revelation 2 and 3, the two women of Revelation 12 and 17, and the various personalities of Hebrews 1 through 7 compared and contrasted with Christ, who is "better."

Recurrence. The reiteration of similar or identical words or phrases is known as recurrence. The repetition of the number "seven" in Revelation, the word "believe" in John, and the word "holy" in Leviticus are illustrations of this principle. The two accounts of creation in Genesis 1 and 2, the threefold picture of the lost sinner in Luke 15, and the three different key words found in Revelation show continuity in the law of recurrence by the use of similar ideas.

Continuity. The essentially uninterrupted treatment of an

idea or subject (such as the Messianic concept in Mark) or the description of a series of events (such as the seven seals of Revelation) illustrates the law of continuity.

Crux. The crux of a narrative is that pivotal set of events which changes the succeeding course of action, such as the crucial events of Esther 4.

Climax. Climax is an arrangement of events, ideas, or propositions in which each occurrence rises above its predecessor in impressiveness or force. Esther 9 is a good illustration of the law of climax. The crucial point in Esther 4 is one event in the series which leads toward the climax in Chapter 9.

Cause and effect. The progression from cause to effect is illustrated by Romans 1:18-32; 1 Corinthians 11:27-32; 2 Thessalonians 2:8-12; and Revelation 13:11-18. The progression from effect to cause is illustrated by John 5:1-18; 9:1-41; Romans 8:18-30; and Revelation 4:4-11; 7:13-17; 14:1-5.

Means to an end. Means is the instrumentality in bringing about a desired end. This involves the idea of purpose. John 20: 30, 31 is an excellent example of this law, for it states that the author chose to record certain signs as a means of accomplishing his purpose. This law is also illustrated in Revelation 6— 18, where the Great Tribulation is described as a means of awakening man to his need of a vital experience with Christ, and also a means of purging the earth in preparation for the millennial reign of Christ. Since the means have a causal relation to the ends, this law is similar to that of cause and effect.

Summary. The use of an abridgment or summary either before or after a unit of material is exemplified by John's prologue (1:1-18) and Revelation 11:15-19.

Problem-solution. The use of questions and answers or problems and solutions is illustrated in Romans 6 and 7 and in Revelation 7:13-17.

Consistency. Since truth is a consistent unity free of contradictions, the reader should expect to find harmony in all the teachings of the Scripture. For example, the records of the inscription on the Cross of Christ as given by the four Gospel writers are complementary rather than contradictory. Paul's instructions to women about praying and prophesying must be interpreted in harmony with his instructions about church decorum and order (1 Cor. 11:1-16; 14:33-40).

The author's structural selectivity

An author also reveals his point of view by selecting those ideas or events which contribute to his overall objective. For example, John's selection of seven specific churches of Asia Minor out of a possible five hundred that existed in John's day (Rev. 2, 3) not only shows contrast and comparison but a definite plan in the structure of the book. The omission of the other churches shows that these seven represent the church universal (since the number seven in Scripture often signifies completeness).

Quantitative selectivity. Often a biblical writer uses quantitative selectivity and *the law of proportion.* With this principle the author proportions his material to the significance of the message. For example, only the first eleven chapters of Genesis are devoted to the beginnings of the whole world and the entire human race, though this period covers many generations. The last thirty-nine chapters deal with only one family and span only four generations. The author is obviously calling our special attention to the Hebrew nation by showing how God has singled out this one family in order to accomplish through them what could not be realized through the human race as a whole.

Qualitative selectivity. When the author selects events or ideas that emphasize a *single event* or a *single idea,* we should ask the following questions:

1. Why did the author include this particular event or idea?
2. Why did the author place this event or idea in this particular context?
3. What does this event or idea contribute to the progress of the book?
4. What is the relation of this event or idea to the surrounding events or ideas?

The selection of only seven out of a possible five hundred churches in Asia Minor (Rev. 2, 3) is an example of this kind of selectivity.

The author's personal identity

Many of the early church's problems with biblical authorship and canonicity arose because the early believers did not understand the Book of Revelation. Though it is not my purpose to discuss in detail the problems of special biblical introduction, I would like to make a few observations about the authorship, occasion, date, design, and destination of Revelation.

According to his own fourfold testimony, the author of Revelation was John (1:1, 4, 9; 22:8). That he was John the Apostle is well attested externally by both the eastern and western church fathers.[2] The book was written at the direct command of the Lord (1:10-13) for the purpose of meeting the needs of persecuted churches of that day. This purpose is found in the very first verse—"to show unto his slaves the things which must shortly come to pass." This purpose is accomplished by John's emphasis upon the Person of Christ.

Some claim that John wrote Revelation during the time of Nero (A.D. 68-69), but the majority of recent expositors hold that the book was written A.D. 95-96 under the reign of Domitian. "This view accords with the fact that the persecution under Domitian, unlike that of Nero, was due to the refusal of the Christians to worship the emperor; cf. 1:9 and a possible anticipatory fulfillment in 13:9, 10, 11, 12."[3] I personally favor the date of A.D. 95.

SUMMARY

We have glanced at the plan of God for the ages in order to help us appreciate the consummation of the ages in Revelation. The actual study of the book itself will fill out many details of the present and future conflict between good and evil. It will also provide a factual basis for the hope of the imminent return of Christ.

The physical, spiritual, and mental preparation which we

---

[2]/See Henry Clarence Thiessen, *Introduction to the New Testament* (Grand Rapids: Wm. B. Eerdmans Publishing Company, 1950), pp. 317-320.

[3]/Thiessen, *op. cit.,* p. 323.

have recommended for the study of Revelation is equally important in studying any other book of the Bible. We will make further study suggestions later, including a sheet of instructions at the beginning of each chapter. We urge you to follow these instructions carefully and finish your independent study in each case before reading the remainder of each chapter.

2

SETTING UP THE GREAT PROJECTOR

Read John 12:20, 21 as your devotional preparation, asking the Lord to give you the same motive as those converted Greeks who said, "We would see Jesus." This book is not a revelation of Saint John but a revelation of Jesus Christ, so above all *see Jesus!*

Now begin looking. Read the entire Book of Revelation at *one sitting.* Read quickly to get a bird's-eye view of the whole. From your survey:

1. Find the major divisions of the book—biographical, geographical, historical, chronological, logical, or ideological.
2. List tentative names for these major divisions, parallel in form and in thought. Revise these as you see more clearly.
3. What is the inspired title of the Book of Revelation?
4. What are the key verses of the book?
5. What are the key words used in the book?
6. What is the purpose of the book?
7. What are the names and characteristics of the recipients?

8. List the characteristics of the book—general and specific.
9. Compare and contrast Revelation with the Book of Daniel.

You may need to survey the whole book several times in order to get the proper perspective. Remember to use your pencil and paper to record observations. Do not use any helps at this point—not even the following pages of discussion. Give the book a chance to speak to you firsthand.

After you have exhausted the possibilities of independent study, read the rest of this chapter.

CHRIST IN THE COMPOSITION

To understand the Revelation of Jesus Christ is becoming increasingly important for those of us living in the twentieth century. To discover what the book really says we must consistently and conscientiously apply the scientific methods of inductive Bible study explained in the preceding chapter. A sincere and honest investigation of Revelation will lead us to a wholehearted, active allegiance to Christ and his program today. Revelation is the only book in the whole Bible that gives a full chronological picture of future events, and it relates them all to Christ. Wherever the Revelation is supplemented by Daniel we have almost all the details for building a system of eschatology. All other prophetical passages are mere glimpses in comparison with the Revelation, yet many current theories of prophecy are based mainly on these glimpses rather than on the only complete unveiling in existence—the Book of Revelation.

Framework

Christ is the great subject and center of the Revelation. The very title itself, "The Revelation of Jesus Christ," shows Christ in sharp focus. He is central in the churches (1:9—3:22), central in the conflict (4:1—16:21), central in the conquest (17:1—20:15), and central in the consummation (21:1—22:5).

In the prologue (1:1-8) Christ corresponds and in the epilogue (22:6-21) he calls. In both the prologue and epilogue his coming is announced five times. So the Revelation is not simply a prediction of divine judgments on the wicked or of the final triumph of the righteous, but an unveiling of Christ himself in his Person, offices, and future administrations.

Vocabulary

The thinking reader will be struck by the marked difference between the style and composition of John's Revelation and that of his Gospel and Epistles. The style of Greek in the Revelation seems entirely different from the style in any of John's other works. And this distinction is noticeable even in English translations. The reason for the difference in style is remarkable. In a very unique sense the Revelation was composed not by John at all but by Jesus Christ himself. This unique type of inspiration is easily discernible in even the smallest detail of the composition. For example, Ivan Panin discovered long ago that there are a total of 888 words (the mark of Christ) and that the 666th word in that vocabulary is *cháragma* (the mark of the Beast)! The Greeks had two important systems of numerals beside the primitive plan of repeating single strokes. The first system was based on the initial letters of numeral names, but as early as the third century before Christ another system came into use. It consisted in assigning nine letters of the Greek alphabet to numbers 1 through 9, nine letters to multiples of 10 up to 90, and nine letters to multiples of 100 up to 900. Because the Greek alphabet contains only 24 letters, three more were added: the Phoenician *vau* (shaped like our letter "F"), *koph* or *qoph* (shaped somewhat like our letter "Q"), and a character known in modern times as *sampi* (originally somewhat similar to the Greek Π tipped about 45° to the right.)[1]

The Greek word for JESUS is 'ΙΗΣΟΥΣ, and the total numerical value of these letters is 888. Is this another indication that this book is a Revelation of Jesus Christ? Only divine

---

[1]/*Encyclopedia Britannica,* 14th Edition, Vol. 16, pp. 611, 612.

GREEK SYSTEM OF NUMBERING INTRODUCED ABOUT 300 B.C.

	A	B	Γ	Δ	E	(F)	Z	H	Θ
Units	1	2	3	4	5	6	7	8	9

	I	K	Λ	M	N	Ξ	O	Π	(Q)
Tens	10	20	30	40	50	60	70	80	90

	P	Σ	T	Y	Φ	X	Ψ	Ω	(&)
Hundreds	100	200	300	400	500	600	700	800	900

The thousands were often indicated by placing a bar to the left of the above numerals thus:

/A = 1000   /B = 2000   /I = 10,000   /Σ = 200,000

---

inspiration could have been responsible for such intricate details and accuracy.

The very structure of the book discloses its unique origin. At every main division John says, "I was in the Spirit," and he reveals the place and circumstance under which he listened to Jesus Christ give this message. This book is not colored by John's personality, as is true with all other books of the Bible and their human "authors." Because the subject matter of Revelation is not native to the human mind, its wording is far beyond the power of human creativeness. Yet Christ, the real author, has written in such a way that man with the help of the Holy Spirit can understand this message about the Son of God.

One important secret in unfolding the Revelation is to understand John's use of key words for indicating symbolism. These are in three groups: *sign* or *signify*, *wonder* or *wonderful*, and *mystery*. Make a reference list of these words and try to see the significance of each in its context.

Characteristics

Every characteristic of the Revelation is consistent with the author's primary purpose of maintaining his focus on Christ.

The book's unity of structure is shown by John's emphasis on the Person of Christ in virtually every chapter. The repetition of "I was in the Spirit" gives the cue for the biographical or Christological divisions. The overall unity of Revelation is also shown by its emphasis on human redemption, the coming of Christ, the sovereignty of God, and the coming kingdom.

Revelation is chronological, historical, and prophetical. Although written in figurative language and filled with symbolical representations, much of the language of Revelation is literal and concrete. There are visions, judgments, and blessings. The structure is numerical, and the subject matter is arranged in sections and blocks. Christ is presented as the faithful witness, the firstborn of the dead, and the ruler of the kings of the earth. These very designations indicate sectional divisions. The reader should attempt to correlate all these cues in order to get the complete viewpoint of the author.

CHRIST IN THE CHRONOLOGY

Is the book chronological? If so, does the chronology center around Christ? Yes, the Revelation contains a definite order of events, beginning with "the things which thou sawest" and ending with the descent to earth of the city of God. Just as in any other type of narrative writing, there is an overlapping of events in their time order. Most interpreters agree on the time-frame of the first three chapters, but how shall the remainder of the book be interpreted? The following are some of the possible theories of interpretation.

The Preterist View

The preterist believes that the symbolism in Revelation applies only to the era in which it was written. For example, the preterist regards the beast in Revelation 13 as simply a figurative description of the contemporary Roman emperor, and not the future Antichrist. In this view John was simply expressing his moral indignation about the abuses of his own day when he spoke about future judgment. This view rejects all future fulfillment of prophecy and has been accepted by the majority of liberal scholars.

The first systematic presentation of the preterist view-point came from Alcazar, a Jesuit friar of the early seventeenth century. Others are Sir William Ramsay, Shailer Matthews, Moses Stuart, Bossuet, Grotius, Hammond, Wetstein, Eichhorn, Ewald, DeWette, Lucke, and Charles M. Laymon (preterist and symbolical views).

One strength of this viewpoint is its stress on the historical background of Revelation. As Ramsay has shown, the meaning of the letters to the seven churches becomes much clearer when we learn about the beginnings and development of the seven Asian cities in which these churches were located.

The major weakness of this viewpoint is the explicit declaration of Revelation 4:1 that certain events must "come to pass *hereafter*." The preterist is unable to account for the future predictions of Revelation 4 through 22.

The Idealist View

The idealist view, known also as the spiritualist view or the symbolic view, is closely allied with the preterist school. It considers Revelation to be only a symbolic representation of that unending conflict of good and evil which persists in every age. It holds that these symbols cannot be identified with any actual historical events, but simply represent ideals or trends. Judgment day comes whenever a great moral issue is decided. There is no predictive prophecy and no final climax, such as the reign of Christ on a visible throne—only the vague ultimate triumph of righteousness. This school of interpretation is represented by Raymond Calkins in his *The Social Message of the Book of Revelation* and by Charles M. Laymon's *The Book of Revelation*. Others are W. Boyd Carpenter and Isaac Williams.

The Synchronous View

The synchronous view, known also as the cyclical or topical view, sees the visions of Revelation starting at various points but all focusing on the final judgment and eternal triumph. The visions present lines or vistas rather than a series of chronological events. Revelation covers the history of

Christianity in the world until the last day, but not in chronological order. The various visions run parallel to a great extent. Representatives of this school are Frederick Brodie, William Frederick Roadhouse, and Richard Charles Henry Lenski.

The Historist View

The historist view, sometimes known as the continuous or continuous-historical view, holds that Revelation outlines in symbolic form the entire course of the history of the church from Pentecost (or possibly the close of the first century) to the second advent of Christ (or possibly the end of time). By this interpretation the various series of churches, seals, trumpets, and bowls are made to represent such events as the breakup of the Roman empire and the Mohammedan invasion. These identifications have led to strained interpretations in order to preserve the proper sequence, with much disagreement among the historists. This failure of exact identification is one of the major weaknesses of this system of thought. A second weakness is the stress on the development of the church in western Europe, with little notice of the East. It makes the book merely an interpretation of history and not a manifestation of Jesus Christ.

In spite of these weaknesses there have been many champions of this theory in the ranks of evangelical Christians, from the Reformation down to modern times. Among these are Luther, Zwingli, Knox, Bullinger, Sir Isaac Newton, Bickersteth, Ellicott, Mede, Brightman, Woodhouse, Cunningham, Birks, Barnes, David Brown, H. Guinness, Hengstenberg, Dean Alford, A. J. Gordon, A. B. Simpson, A. R. Fausett, Matthew Henry, and C. Anderson Scott.

The Futurist View

The futurist generally believes that all the visions from Revelation 4:1 to the end of the book are to be fulfilled in a period immediately preceding and following the second coming of Christ. The reason for the view is found in comparing Revelation 1:1, 19 with 4:1. The first three chapters apply to the day in which the book was written, or else the seven churches of Asia represent seven eras of church history which span the period from the apostolic age to the return of Christ. Beginning with 4:1, "the things which must come to pass here- after," the remainder of the book deals with events that will take place during the Great Tribulation and into the eternal ages. The events of the Apocalypse are interpreted as literally as possible. Expositors who hold this view are John Quincy Adams, J. Sidlow Baxter, Arno C. Gaebelein, Norman B. Har- rison, William G. Heslop, Harry Allan Ironside, Clarence Larkin, Willis Mead, William R. Newell, Thomas Newberry, Ford C. Ottman, Joseph Augustus Seiss, D. M. Stearns, J. L. Thompson, C. I. Scofield, Burgh, Maitland, Benjamin Newton, Todd, and Merrill C. Tenney. There are also extreme futurists, such as Kelly and some Irish authors, who place even the first three chapters of Revelation into the future.

Which of these five chronological schemes is correct? Which one makes Christ most central? As to the *preterist* view, it is true that John referred to certain events of his day, since the seven churches of Asia were actual geographical real- ities, but it is *not* true that we are not approaching a final judgment and that the book contains no predictive prophecy. Revelation is far more than an uninspired historical document!

As to the *idealist* view, Revelation does picture a struggle between good and evil, but this struggle is personalized and can be identified with historic and prophetic events. Illustrations are the churches of Asia, the tribulation judgments, the seven personages, the millennial age, and the personal reign of Christ.

As to the *synchronous* view, there is indeed a focal point in all the predictive prophecy in Revelation—the revelation of Christ as King of Kings and Lord of Lords—but there is also a definite chronological arrangement of the prophecies. Some of the chapters do run parallel, but this is true of *any* account of historical or prophetical events.

As to the *historist* view, it is true that certain events of church history are predicted by the seven churches, but it is not correct to place the Great Tribulation judgments in the past.

As to the *futurist* view, which seems closer to the truth, it is true that everything from Revelation 4:1 to the end of the book is still future, but because of the shifting line between Philadelphia and Laodicea, some of Chapter 3 must also be considered part of the still-future Great Tribulation. In other words, the Laodicean church not only represents a condition which has existed from the first century, but this condition of lukewarmness will be the chief characteristic of religious conditions at the beginning of the Great Tribulation period. Also, the symbols of the two women in Chapters 12 and 17 cannot be *wholly* confined to the future even though Revelation deals *primarily* with their future culmination. The overall picture will become clearer as the great projector is focused on later details of the visions. Though the Christ that is revealed in Revelation is far more important than any chronology, it should be obvious that the Revelation which Jesus Christ showed his slaves must be as rational as its ultimate Author. If the content of the book is a revelation, and if its ultimate source is God the Father, then nothing but an orderly presentation can be possible.

The first two key verses of Revelation (1:19, 20) unlock the chronological plan of the book, prepare the reader for the figurative interpretation of certain symbols, and place Christ in the center of the churches. The key phrase, which is repeated four times (1:10; 4:2; 17:3; 21:10), unlocks the biographical or Christological plan of the book, making Christ central in his revelation. As the whole plan of the book unfolds we will continue to see Christ in the chronology!

SUMMARY

When we discover Christ in the very composition of the Revelation, we see that he is central in the framework, the vocabulary, and every other characteristic of the book. Our brief survey of the different interpretations of the chronology of Revelation shows that the futuristic view, with certain modifications, is the most tenable. We are now ready to focus the projector on the details of the first chapter of Revelation.

PART TWO

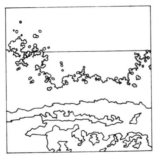

CHRIST
IN THE CHURCHES

3

CHRIST THE CENTER OF INTEREST

Revelation 1

INSTRUCTIONS FOR STUDYING REVELATION 1

Read Revelation 22:6-21 as your devotional approach, asking the Lord to help you see the prologue (1:1-8) in the light of the epilogue (22:6-21). Now focus your attention on Chapter 1, taking special notice of the first eight verses. Remember to *study independently* before reading the following pages.

Study Project Number 1 Compare and contrast the references to the imminence of Christ's coming in the prologue and epilogue. How many references do you find in each? Use either horizontal or vertical columns to scan all the references.[1] Do all these references say the same thing? If not, what are their different emphases? Is there continuity? If so, does the author follow any plan of development? Is there a unifying idea behind each group? What is the relation between the groups?

Study Project Number 2 What other comparisons and contrasts do you see between the prologue and epilogue? In order to see these more clearly, why not choose a title for each paragraph (or verse)? You may want to divide some of the

---

[1]/See Appendix 2 for a sample vertical chart.

SAMPLE FORM OF A PARAGRAPH CHART

THE REVELATION OF JESUS CHRIST

Author:
Purpose:
Date:
Recipients:
Source:
Theme:
Signature:
Key Verses:
Key Sentence:
Key Words:

Paragraph
headings
(the word "title"
could be used
for the first
and "purpose"
for the
second)

Put Any Other Suggestions
for Dividing the Book Here

| Verse numbers | 1 | 2 | 3 | 4 | 5 | 7 | 8 | 9 | 12 | 19 | 1 | 8 | 12 | 18 |

Chapter numbers 1   NAMES OF SEGMENTS   2

NAMES OF SUB-SECTIONS

NAMES OF SECTIONS

NAMES OF DIVISIONS

paragraphs. As you proceed you will begin to see the correlation between the two groups of paragraphs. The next step will be to group each set together by giving each segment a name. These paragraph titles, as well as the name for the first segment of the prologue, may be used to begin your paragraph chart right away.

Study Project Number 3 Now focus your attention on the entire first chapter. List and quote the references to the different Persons of the Godhead, classifying them under their respective persons and noting significant observations. Then continue working on your paragraph chart.

Read Revelation 1 over again and try stating the theme of the second segment. Does your theme give Christ his rightful place? What is the relationship between the segments? What does the author accomplish in Chapter 1? Compare the structure of Revelation 1 with that of John 1.

Now list five to ten observations on Revelation 1, indicating the significance of each. Do not let these observations overlap Study Projects 1 through 3.

What have you learned in this study by way of new spiritual values? What practical applications can you make to your own life? After exhausting all the possibilities of independent study, read the rest of this chapter.

NOTES ON REVELATION 1

CHRIST IN THE PROLOGUE (1:1-8)

The central emphasis of the prologue is on Christ the Coming One; each of the five references in these eight verses indicates that his coming is imminent. But each reference also has an additional emphasis.

Verse 1 answers the question *what?* and informs us that *certain things must shortly come to pass.* These events include all the prophecies of the entire Apocalypse, and the word "shortly" refutes the historical interpretation.

Verse 3 answers the question *when?* by telling us that the time is *at hand.* If the time was near in the year 95, how much more eagerly can we look for the coming of our Lord in our own age!

Verse 4 answers the question *why?* This idea is expressed by the present substantial restrictive participle (*ho erchómenos,* the Coming One). The One who is coming is the Father. He is coming in the Person of Christ for the very special purpose of bringing his kingdom to its glorious consummation.

Verse 7 answers the question *how?* by telling us that Christ is coming openly and with the clouds—"Behold, he cometh *with clouds;* and every eye shall see him, and they that pierced him; and all the tribes of the earth shall mourn over him." The effect of his coming will be repentance and salvation, especially among the Jews. "I will pour upon the house of David, and upon the inhabitants of Jerusalem, the spirit of grace and of supplication," said Jehovah, "and they shall look unto me whom they have pierced; and they shall mourn for him, as one mourneth for his only son, and shall be in bitterness for him, as one that is in bitterness for his firstborn" (Zech. 12:10). Christ repeats this idea in his prophetical discourse: "And then shall appear the sign of the Son of man in heaven; and then shall all the tribes of the earth mourn, and they shall see the Son of man coming on the clouds of heaven with power and great glory" (Matt. 24:30).

Verse 8 answers the question *who?* by showing that Christ *the Almighty* is the Coming One! He is God of Very God, co-equal with the Father. Jesus said, "I and my Father are one," and since the neuter *hen* is used for "one," the meaning is "one in essence." If the masculine had been used, the meaning would have been that the Father and the Son were to be considered as one Person. Since they are actually two personalities, we can see the wisdom of inspiration in choosing even the correct gender.

The Purpose (1:1, 2)

The entire Book of Revelation, and especially Chapter 1, is a disclosure which God intended Jesus Christ to reveal to his slaves. The independent Greek nominative *apokálupsis*[2] sug-

---

[2]/*Apokálupsis* is anarthrous (has no article), but this noun is made

gests the title while the objective genitive "of Jesus Christ"[3] indicates the One who is to be unveiled in this one great showing. In other words, the Person who *shows* the Revelation is the same Person to be revealed!

The word for servant here is really "slave" (*doúlos*), a servile word related to "lord" (*kúrios*) or "despot" (*despótēs*).[4] The word is used fourteen times in Revelation and many times in the other books of the New Testament. For example, Paul calls himself a slave of Jesus Christ in the first verses of Romans and Titus. The significance of this word here in Revelation is that only those people who are abandoned to the will of Jesus Christ as Lord and Master qualify for this one great disclosure. This means that if we are to really understand what Jesus Christ is saying in the Revelation, we must be prepared by the spirit of prayer, the Spirit of truth, and the spirit of obedience.

This Revelation was sent and signified (*sēmaínō*)[5] by Christ's angel—"And he sent and signified it by his angel unto his servant John."[6] The word of this angel formed the con-

definite by the genitive ("of Jesus Christ") and by the relative clause ("which God gave him to show unto his slaves"). In fact, the absence of the article stresses the *quality* or *character* of the Revelation.

3/Commentators differ here, but of the twelve uses of *apokálupsis* in the New Testament (Luke 2:32; Rom. 2:5; 8:19; 16:25; 1 Cor. 1:7; 2 Cor. 12:1; Gal. 1:12; 2 Thess. 1:7; 1 Pet. 1:7, 13; 4:13; Rev. 1:1) it is doubtful that any are subjective genitives.

4/Five other words are listed by Richard Chenevix Trench in his *Synonyms of the New Testament* (Grand Rapids: Wm. B. Eerdmans Publishing Co., 1960), pp. 30-34. *Oikétēs* is often equivalent to *doúlos* (as in 1 Pet. 2:18), but it does not bring out and emphasize the servile relations so strongly. *Oikétēs* is someone of the household or family, though not by birth. *Therápōn* is used only in Heb. 3:5, of Moses, and it relates to voluntary service and a more confidential position. *Oikonómos* is also a voluntary steward in God's house (Num. 12:6-8). *Diákonos* represents a servant in his activity, with emphasis on his *work* (Eph. 3:7; Col. 1:23; 2 Cor. 3:6) rather than his relation to a person. *Huperétēs* is a military term for temple guard, under-officer, and assistant. He was originally the rower, as distinguished from the soldier, on board a war-galley; then the subordinate official who waited to accomplish the behests of his superior, as the orderly who attends the commander in war; and then the herald who carried a solemn message. Mark was a *huperétēs* to Paul and Barnabas (Acts 13:5).

5/*Sēmaínō*, "to make known by signs and symbols," is related to *sēmeíon*, "sign," used in 12:1, 3; 13:13, 14; 15:1; 16:14; 19:20.

6/Cf. Rev. 18:21; 19:9, 10; 22:8, 9.

nection between John's senses and the things of Christ; the angel "televised" future events and replayed them to John.[7] The message was not modified by the angel; he simply transmitted the message like the operator of a movie projector. So in the final analysis it was Christ himself who did the "showing."

A revelation is the unveiling of a mystery which could never be discovered by the unaided human mind. The ultimate source of this revelation is God the Father, and the line of transmission is as follows: from God the Father, to Jesus Christ, to Christ's slave (John), to all other slaves of Christ. Lord, help us to qualify as slaves!

The Blessing (1:3)

The first of seven "blesseds" is found here in the prologue, and this blessing is extended to

1. The person *reading* (aloud), and
2. The persons *hearing* the words of the prophecy, and
3. The persons *keeping* (strictly) the things which are written therein.

Since only one copy of the Revelation was sent to each of the seven churches, and since ancient handwritten manuscripts were difficult to read, the author had in mind the public reading and hearing of the words. The neglect of this marvelous book in church services today accounts for the absence of its promised blessing.[8] How can the pastor expect his people to "keep" the words of this prophecy without hearing them? And how can the people hear unless the words are read? It is not enough to say, "They can read for themselves," for the average person has a closed mind to the Revelation because he finds it difficult to understand. Lord, help us, like Ezra, to read it and give the sense![9]

The Address (1:4, 5a)

Even though there were many Christian churches in Asia

7/Cf. Heb. 1:14; Matt. 4:8.
8/Cf. 1 Tim. 4:13.
9/Neh. 8:8.

Minor at the time of John's vision,[10] he was told to write only to the seven churches designated in verses 4, 11, and 20. Since verses 1–3 indicate that the ultimate source of this Revelation is God himself, there is no need for John to call himself an apostle in order to get a hearing. Since John recorded what he actually saw, and since he was also told exactly what to write, we can be sure of "inspiration plus" in the Book of Revelation!

From the One who is and who was and who is coming (1:4)

The designation "from him who is and who was and who is to come" is found only in Revelation. In this verse the wording applies to the Father, but in verse 8 Jesus uses the same words in referring to his own equality with the Father.[11] The whole designation that follows "from" would ordinarily be in the ablative case, but here the indeclinable noun is used because the Greek language contained no adequate expression of eternity. "This is not ignorance, but intelligence working with a medium of language that lags in its forms and has gaps."[12] The nearest English counterpart would be "the Being One and the Was One and the Coming One." What we see in this phrase is the Eternal and Absolute One—the self-existent, incomprehensible, infinite, unapproachable Father of lights and Source of all being.

From the seven spirits who are before his throne (1:4)

The second source of the greeting is the Holy Spirit in all his sevenfold perfection. He is the One who is represented in Revelation 4:5 as the seven lamps of the fire burning before the throne. So the "seven" of Spirit and the "seven" of the church agree, indicating completeness or perfection.[13]

In Isaiah 11:2 the Spirit rests upon Christ in his governmental offices in a sevenfold way: (1) the spirit of Jehovah

---

10/W. M. Ramsay, *The Letters to the Seven Churches of Asia* (Grand Rapids: Baker Book House, 1963 reprint), pp. 176, 177.

11/Cf. 4:8; 11:17; 16:5; see also John 10:30; 14:9, 10.

12/Richard Charles Henry Lenski, *The Interpretation of St. John's Revelation* (Minneapolis, Minnesota: Augsburg Publishing House, 1961), pp. 37, 38. Copyright owners by assignment from The Wartburg Press. Reprinted by permission.

13/Cf. Exod. 25:32; Zech. 4:2.

(Deity), (2) the spirit of wisdom, (3) the spirit of understanding, (4) the spirit of counsel, (5) the spirit of might,
(6) the spirit of knowledge, and (7) the spirit of the fear of
Jehovah. So grace and peace come from the Holy Spirit as well
as from God the Father (1:4).

From Jesus Christ, the Faithful Witness, the Firstborn from the
dead, and the Ruler of the kings of the earth (1:5)

The third source of the greeting is Jesus Christ. Verse 5
gives him three titles which may represent his work on earth
in chronological order. First, he is the faithful witness—not
only during his earthly ministry[14] but also in the present
revelation (3:14). Second, he is the "firstborn from the dead."
This designation clearly refers to Christ's resurrection.[15] Christ
is the firstborn from the dead because all others who were
raised before him (such as Lazarus) died again. The word
"firstborn" refers to rank and divine personal dignity, as in
Colossians 1:15—"the firstborn of all creation." This does
not for a moment mean that Christ is a created being. Since
Christ "was raised again for our justification" (Rom. 4:25),
this second title presents him as our Redeemer. The third
title, "the ruler of the kings of the earth," refers to the consummation of Christ's earthly work, when he will rule over
every dignitary in the world. Can you correlate these three titles
with the general structure of the book?

The Ascription (1:5b, 6)

The opening doxology is filled with adoration for the Son
and for the Father. This praise springs from Christ's constant
love for us (expressed by the present participle) and from the
once-for-all loosing of our sins by his blood (expressed by the
aorist participle).

The finite verb "made" (*epóiēsen*, v. 6) which follows the
two participles does not indicate faulty grammar but a special emphasis on the third statement: "Unto the One loving us
and loosing us from our sins in connection with his blood—

14/John 7:7; 18:37; 1 Tim. 6:13.
15/1 Cor. 15:20; Acts 2:32, 33.

and *he made us a kingdom, priests to his God and Father.*"[16] What Israel was to be (and finally will be) Christ has made *us* to be. By this means the King establishes his own kingdom forever. Though eternity is not a mere succession of time, the only way to express "forever" in Greek is to pluralize the greatest term for time, the eon, and then multiply it by its own plural—*eis tous aiō'nas tōn aiō'nōn* ("into the ages of the ages"). So this ascription of praise is directed both to the Son and to the Father, who are separate in personality but single in essence, purpose, and work.

The Theme (1:7)

Before recording his first vision, John states the summary theme and appends Christ's own signature. The mention of a kingdom and priests suggests the climax which must precede these realities. Just as the prologue to John's Gospel summarizes the entire drama of redemption which follows, so the prologue to Revelation (especially verse 7) sweeps through to the very climax of the book: "Behold, he is coming with the clouds, and every eye shall see him, and they that pierced him; and all of the tribes of the earth shall beat themselves in mourning over him." Even though John omits the name of the coming One, it seems clear that he is the Jesus Christ of the preceding verses and the same Person who comes with clouds in Acts 1:9. This composite picture provides no details of the rapture, Tribulation, and revelation, for these details will be revealed in the chapters which follow. Instead, Revelation 1:7 emphasizes the *fact* of his coming, the *universality* of his coming ("every eye shall see him"), and the *effect* of his coming ("all the tribes of the earth shall mourn over him"). This is an exact fulfillment of Matthew 24:27-31.[17]

This great prophecy is then sealed with Christ's own signature: "I am . . . the Almighty" (verse 8). So here Christ declares himself to be all that the Father is, since there is no higher name than "the Almighty." This means that everything is subjected to Christ. Hallelujah!

16/Cf. 5:10; 1 Pet. 2:9; Exod. 19:6.
17/Cf. Zech. 14:1-5; Isa. 2:19.

CHRIST AS THE LIVING ONE (1:9-20)

The Revelation proper now begins with a vision of Christ himself. This first vision really extends through Chapter 3, for Christ is seen "in the midst of the candlesticks" (1:13). John represents himself here as a personal witness rather than an apostle,[18] and he tells us that this great revelation happened on a certain Sunday—*en tē kuriakē hēméra* (on the Lord's day)[19]—approximately A.D. 95, near the end of the reign of the Emperor Domitian (A.D. 81-96). The place was the Isle of Patmos, opposite the southern coast of Roman provincial Asia. Since this showing is only for slaves, only those people who make Christ's will their own will are able to see everything that is to be seen. In other words, the spectator must belong to Christ, who bought him with the price of his blood, and he must recognize Christ as his Lord by offering him absolute obedience and submissive service. If we would see Jesus, we must be in the Spirit. If we would hear what John heard, we must be led by the Holy Spirit, who prepares our hearts and our minds.

The Recipients (1:9-11)

Christ first appears in this vision as "the great voice like a trumpet," and his commands are:
1. Write what you see in a book.
2. Send it to the seven churches.

The words which follow these commands belong to the church age (which is represented by the seven churches of Asia) and not to Israel or to the day of the Lord. Seven is the number of completeness, and here it designates the whole Christian body on earth at that time as well as all the succeeding periods of church history.

The Son of Man (1:12-18)

The "one like unto a son of man" is Christ himself, and it

18/Dan. 7:15; 8:1; 9:2; Rev. 22:8.
19/In the New Testament, the word occurs only here and in 1 Cor. 11:20. It has no reference to the day of the Lord (*hēméra kuríou*) as in 2 Pet. 3:10.

is he who gives light to the lampstands or candlesticks. Here John sees the glorified Lord just as he saw him on the Mount of Transfiguration, and the description is as follows.

"One like unto a son of man" (1:13).

When Christ took the form of a man at the time of his nativity, he forever united his Deity with humanity. He is still the God-man, and his glorified body is a pattern of what his saints will be like when the "change" comes. So Christ is both a man and more than a man. In this chapter of Revelation he has the glory that he possessed with the Father before the world began, but he is still Godhead embodied in humanity.

"Clothed with a garment down to the foot, and girt about at the breasts with a golden girdle" (1:13).

What an impressive sight! The long, flowing vestment speaks of modesty and dignity while the girding at the breast rather than at the waist or hips indicates rest rather than action. His work on earth as a servant has been accomplished. When he cried "It is finished," there was nothing left undone. Just as "a son of man" speaks of humanity, so the gold speaks of Deity.

"His head and his hair were white as white wool, white as snow" (1:14).

Christ's white hair represents holiness rather than aging.[20] The flexible Greek participles (instead of verbs) in verses 13–16 paint the dramatic strokes of the tremendous mystery in highly symbolical language.

"His eyes were as a flame of fire" (1:14).

Here we see the searching, discerning, all-penetrating power before which nothing can hide. This power will soon judge the world, and when those searching eyes read the thoughts of men's hearts at the judgment day, who will be able to stand? Only those whose sins have been cleansed by the precious blood of the Judge himself. Then the loving eyes of the Suffering Servant will be changed into the judging eyes of fire.

20/Cf. Dan. 7:9; Isa. 1:18.

"His feet like unto burnished brass, as if it had been refined in a furnace" (*1:15*).

This glowing gold-bronze represents the intense fire of the furnace of judgment, for "where such feet tread they utterly blast and instantly turn to ashes everything they touch or even approach" (Lenski). "And if the righteous scarcely be saved, where shall the ungodly and the sinner appear?" (1 Pet. 4:18, KJV).

"His voice as the voice of many waters" (1:15).

Here the mighty voice of the Lord shall sound from his habitation with the overwhelming power of a roaring cataract. It will be great enough for all that are in the graves to hear and live.

"He had in his right hand seven stars" (*1:16*).

These seven stars are the ministers or pastors of the seven churches, and are therefore distinct from the candlesticks.[21] Both the pastors of the church as the Lord's messengers and the churches themselves are in the Lord's hand. Thus ministers have a special relation to Christ, for they partake directly of Christ's authority. "If they are unfaithful, none can deliver them out of that hand, but if true to their position, none can touch them or quench their light."[22]

"Out of his mouth proceeded a sharp, two-edged sword" (*1:16*).

The great sword, as tall as a man, would have to be wielded by both hands, but no hand swings this sword. The Word of this Almighty One fulfills the prophecy of Isaiah 11:4 —"He shall smite the earth with the rod of his mouth."

"His countenance was as the sun shineth in his strength" (*1:16*).

The description here is not of the face but of the whole appearance—the sum total of the vision. Here the glory of the Lord is unveiled in all of its majesty and radiance. Little wonder that John reacted to the awful unveiling by falling at

---

[21]/Cf. Dan. 12:3.
[22]/Joseph Augustus Seiss, *The Apocalypse* (Grand Rapids: Zondervan Publishing House, 1869 reprint), p. 41.

Christ's feet as dead! This was no ordinary fear, but a true religious dread and awe. It was the feeling of John's own submergence in the presence of infinite power. This unexplainable element in religion must be experienced in order to be understood.

The hand of grace was laid upon John (1:17), and the great voice became the loving voice of assurance: "Be not fearing!" John's silence indicates his own submergence in the presence of the Transcendent One. It is the emotion of a creature who is submerged and overwhelmed by the One who is supreme above all creatures.

At this point the Lord identifies himself again, and the designation is like a signature and seal placed at the head of the whole Revelation.

1. "I am the First and the Last,
2. And the Living One; and I was dead,
3. And behold, I am alive forevermore,
4. And I have the keys of death and of hades" (1:17, 18).

This signature designates Christ in much the same sublime way as verse 8. There he is the Alpha and the Omega; here he is the First and the Last. There he is the Eternal One; here he is the Living One. There he is the Almighty; here he has the keys of death and hades. In Old Testament times death held the bodies of men and hades held their spirits, but since Christ's death and resurrection hades no longer holds the spirits of God's saints.[23] The death and resurrection of Christ constitute the basis for everything he will accomplish throughout the Revelation, including the casting of death and hades into the lake of fire (20:14).

23/Hades before the ascension of Christ had two divisions with a great gulf between. One was a place of torment for unsaved people, such as the rich man of Luke 16:19-31. Christ called the other division "Abraham's bosom" (Lk. 16:22) and "Paradise" (Lk. 23:43), and here all of the blessed dead were alive, conscious, and comforted. Scriptures such as Eph. 4:8-10; 1 Pet. 3:18-20; 2 Cor. 5:6; 12:4; Psalm 16:10; and Matt. 16:18 seem to indicate that the location of Paradise was transferred at the ascension of Christ, so that during the present church age the saints who die go into the immediate presence of God.

The Explanation (1:19, 20)

The second command to write[24] follows the second signature. In the first command (verse 11) John is told to write "What thou seest." This seems to summarize everything before John sees anything. But in verses 13 and 17 he begins to see, for Christ fills his vision. So "the things which thou sawest" of the second command must refer to the vision from verses 10 through 20. This vision of Christ in Chapter 1 forms the basis for the visions of the present in Chapters 2 and 3, and for those of the future in Chapters 4 through 22. These key verses indicate a definite chronological division of the Revelation. Why not place these divisions along the top of your chart?

The key word "mystery" indicates symbolism, and the mystery of the seven stars is explained as the angels or "messengers" of the seven churches, which are represented by the seven golden candlesticks.

SUMMARY

We have seen that the prologue is really a resumé of the entire Revelation, for it contains the title, the purpose, the witness, the first blessing, the name of the author, the names of the recipients, the source of the vision, the Redeemer, the

---

[24]/There are twelve commands to write and one *not* to write* in the Book of Revelation, as follows:

1:11 "What thou seest, write in a book and send it."
1:19 "Write therefore the things which thou sawest."
2:1 "To the angel of the church in Ephesus write."
2:8 "To the angel of the church in Smyrna write."
2:12 "To the angel of the church in Pergamum write."
2:18 "To the angel of the church in Thyatira write."
3:1 "To the angel of the church in Sardis write."
3:7 "To the angel of the church in Philadelphia write."
3:14 "To the angel of the church in Laodicea write."
14:13 "Write, Blessed are the dead who die in the Lord."
19:9 "Write, Blessed are they that are bidden to the marriage."
21:5 "Write, for these words are faithful and true."
*10:4 "Seal up the things which the seven thunders uttered, and *write them not.*"

theme, the signature, and the five announcements of the imminence of Christ's coming.

The rest of the chapter is a vivid revelation of Christ the Living One, and the explanation of the symbolic candlesticks and stars helps us understand the symbols which appear in the succeeding chapters of Revelation. By keeping our focus on Christ we can explore the further unfolding of the Revelation.

4

CHRIST THE CENTER OF THE CHURCHES

Revelation 2, 3

INSTRUCTIONS FOR STUDYING REVELATION 2 AND 3

Read Matthew 16:13-20 as your devotional approach to this section. Pray for the same Spirit of revelation which was given to Peter. Now pursue your independent study, following the methods suggested in Chapter 1. The following summary of methods and additional suggestions will help you concentrate on the informative second and third chapters of Revelation.

HOW TO STUDY A SECTIONAL UNIT IN A BOOK OF THE BIBLE

First, read the entire section, scrutinizing the meaning as though you were reading it for the first time in your life. Try to grasp exactly what each sentence says, even if it is different from what you had previously thought.

Second, choose a title for each paragraph in the section. Remember that these titles may be descriptive, analytical, or interpretive. Brief, descriptive titles are best for the early stages of your study. Remember to use the paragraph rather than the chapter as your unit of study. Think over your titles until you can remember them in correct sequence without referring to your book or your notes.

Third, study the structural relation of each paragraph to the ones preceding and following it.[1] Ask yourself such questions as

1. Why did the writer put this paragraph in his book?
2. Why did he put it in this particular place in the book?
3. What does this event or idea contribute to the progress of the book?
4. What is the relation of this event or idea to the surrounding events or ideas?

Sometimes the connection is merely chronological, but at other times it is much more than this. Occasionally you will find little obvious connection. If you discover some relationship that you had not noticed before, make a written note of it.

Fourth, when you have finished a segment of paragraphs, apply the above suggestions to the segment as a whole in its relation to the segments preceding and following it. Ask yourself such questions as

1. What does this segment add to the movement of the book?
2. Would the omission of this segment seriously affect the plan of the book? If so, how?

Fifth, state the theme of the segment. You may be able to state the theme in a number of ways, and some of these may be useful for names of segments, subsections, or divisions on your chart. Or you may wish to make an outline which would develop your theme.

Sixth, make a list of five to ten significant observations about the segment. This involves correlating facts and statements so as to get beneath the surface. Then you will begin to see things in the segment that you never saw before. Record the results. Do not let these observations overlap your study up to this point. Remember to keep interpretation to a

---

[1]/See pages 12-14.

minimum at this point, and avoid all applications for the time being.

Just what is an observation? In general, observation is awareness of the particulars of a passage. A meaningful observation includes four things:

1. *The definition and identity of significant terms or words.* For example, "overcometh," which occurs seven times in Revelation 2 and 3, comes from *nikáō,* to conquer, and means to be victor in a battle or contest. Here it is used "of Christians, that hold fast their faith even unto death against the power of their foes and their temptations and persecutions."[2]

2. *The awareness of the structure or relations* which bind these terms into a literary unit, such as phrase, clause, sentence, paragraph, etc. For example, the student will notice that the basic structure of Revelation 2 and 3 is woven around seven messages to the seven churches of Asia. Having noted these paragraphical units, he will then apply the laws of relationship, such as comparison and contrast, to these paragraphs.

3. *The observation of the general literary form,* such as, a) extended discourse or logical literature, which appeals primarily to the intellect; b) narrative prose, which appeals primarily to the imagination and the emotions; c) dramatic prose and poetry, which are emotional in nature; d) parables, which employ the principle of analogy; and e) apocalyptic literature, which is characterized by symbolism, visions, and predictions. The literary form of Revelation 2 and 3 is epistolary or discursive, but it also has an apocalyptic element. We should therefore be concerned about the location, characteristics, and problems of the recipients; the occasion, purpose, literary features, leading ideas, and central truths of the letters; the interpretation of the symbols; and the relation of the prophetic elements to the whole book.

---

[2]/Joseph Henry Thayer, *Greek-English Lexicon of the New Testament* (New York: American Book Company, 1889), p. 426.

4. *The consideration of atmosphere or spirit of the passage.* This helps us determine the author's mind and spirit. Is he joyful or sorrowful? Is he optimistic or pessimistic? Does he have a spirit of thanksgiving or disappointment? Is he prone to commend or condemn? Is he humble or boastful? Does he manifest tenderness or abruptness? Does he have a sense of urgency or unconcern? Or is there a combination of various moods?

These four elements need not be noted separately, since all four will probably be intermingled in your observations.

Seventh, if you have not already done so in the previous steps, study the persons and places mentioned. If places or journeys are prominent, as in the Book of Acts, draw a rough map indicating significant locations. A map of Asia Minor which identifies the seven cities in Revelation 2 and 3 would be especially helpful.

Eighth, record any questions and difficulties that you encountered in your study and discuss these with your instructor or pastor.

Ninth, you are now ready for interpretation. The basic problem is one of re-creation. This process changes the written word into the living word, identifying the interpreter with the experiences of the writer of the book. This imaginative projection of our own consciousness into someone else's is called "empathy" and is especially important in studying the Revelation. Until we can sit with John in exile on the Isle of Patmos and go with him through the open door to the very throne of heaven, we will never become a true interpreter of Revelation.

There are three basic steps in the interpretive process—interpretive questions, interpretive answers, and interpretive integration and summarization.

1. *The interpretive question* is an intermediate step between observation and interpretation. It is either a part of observation or it arises after the observation is made. The interpreter asks such questions as, "What

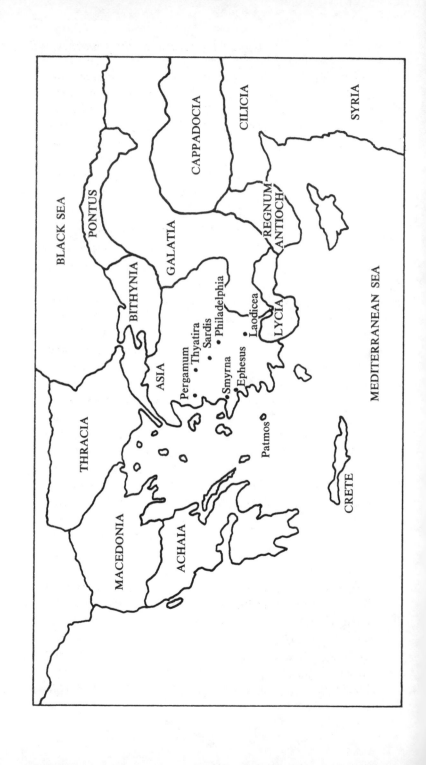

does this mean? Why was this said? Why was it said here? What does it imply? Who or what is involved? How is this accomplished? When is this accomplished? Where is this accomplished?" For example, how many churches did John address? What did he say to these churches? Why did he say something different to each church? Why did he limit his addresses to seven? How did he close each letter? Why don't all the letters end the same way? Is the second advent of Christ mentioned in all seven letters? Why? What does this imply? What is the meaning of "the hour of trial" in 3:10? What is the promise here? What is the implication?

2. *Interpretive answers* are the next step in true exegesis. These answers will be influenced by both subjective and objective factors. Subjectively, the interpreter must have spiritual sense, common sense, and human experience. Objectively, he must be prepared to make a thorough study of the important words of the passage by the use of lexicons, Bible dictionaries, word studies, books of synonyms, and various translations of the Bible. He must pay special attention to the significance of inflections in the original languages; he must note the implications of the contextual relations, both immediate and remote; he must be aware of the implications of the general literary forms, such as parabolic, poetic, and apocalyptic; he must apply the factor of atmosphere in such passages as Romans 9—11; he must determine the author's purpose and viewpoint; he must acquaint himself with historical background material; he must take into account the psychological factors of emotions, attitudes, motives, and aspirations; he must be aware of ideological implications which are never explicitly stated in Scripture, such as the existence of God; he must see progress in revelation from Genesis to Revelation; he must see the essential harmony of the books of the Bible; he must believe in the verbal,

plenary inspiration of the Scriptures as originally given, and yet recognize both the divine source and the human instruments; he must recognize the value of textual or lower criticism in order to ascertain the true reading of the text; and he must investigate the views and interpretations of others as a last and important step in arriving at the true interpretation.

3. *Interpretive integration and summarization* may be done by listing the main truths which have been discovered; by the use of a descriptive title or proposition; by the use of analytical or interpretive paragraph titles in narrative literature; by the making of an analytical, topical, or logical outline of the passage; by writing a paraphrase; by making a chart; or by writing an essay of several paragraphs.

Tenth, the ultimate goal in studying the Scriptures is to make their teachings a vital part of our lives. By reserving application to the end of our study, we are better able to apply what we have learned to our daily Christian living.

STUDY PROJECT NUMBER 4

Make a vertical-column chart of the seven churches in Revelation 2 and 3, following the pattern in Appendix 2. Write the names of the churches at the top of parallel columns, then compare and contrast them by the following divisions at the left margin: *Commission* (to write), *Designation* (of Christ), *Commendation* (of the Church), *Condemnation, Exhortation, Predication, Admonition,* and *Promise.* Quote the Scriptures in full in the appropriate squares and indicate their references. *Be sure to maintain the scriptural sequence of the verses.* Then evaluate the moral quality of each church. Use such terms as *much good, little good, no good, much bad, some bad, little bad, no bad.* Then list five to ten observations based on this study. Remember that the arrangement of the author's material is the cue to his viewpoint. Be sure to incorporate your final chart into one side only of a single sheet of paper.

NOTES ON REVELATION 2, 3

PRELIMINARY OBSERVATIONS

Christ's letters to the seven churches of Asia, like his parables, enjoy the distinction of consisting exclusively of Christ's own words. Although these letters do not precisely follow the epistolary form of the Pauline Epistles, they are in a real sense Epistles of Christ. They are not messages from an absent Lord but sentences of a present Judge. In each case John is the amanuensis and Christ is the Author. These letters are probably the only unabridged records of Christ's addresses which are available to us.

Christ is represented by a different figure in each message, but each designation of Christ is part of the description of the Son of Man in Chapter 1. All except two of the churches (Sardis and Laodicea) receive some praise from Christ, and all except two (Smyrna and Philadelphia) also receive a condemnation. Each message has an exhortation, a prediction, an admonition, and a promise.

These messages were not sent as separate letters to the seven churches but formed part of a complete book or scroll (*biblíon*, 1:11) which was sent to all the churches. Even though each of the seven churches is personally addressed in turn, all seven churches were instructed to read all seven letters together with the rest of the book.

These seven churches are named in a definite order. By noting the location of the seven cities on the map of Asia Minor, you will see that they form a rough circle coincident with the main trade routes of that day. The circle begins at Ephesus and moves northward through Smyrna toward Pergamum, then returns southeast through Thyatira, Sardis, and Philadelphia to Laodicea, finally returning westward to Ephesus. The completing of the circle, together with the total of seven churches (signifying completeness), implies that this group of churches represents the Church universal.

CHRIST'S MESSAGE TO EPHESUS (2:1-7)[3]

Ephesus was the capital of proconsular Asia and a magnificent center of trade on the western coast of Asia Minor. Paul pioneered the church here, and Timothy later continued the work. Ephesus was the home of the Apostle John and was possibly also the last home of Mary the mother of Jesus, since Christ committed her to John at the Cross. It was also the city in which Apollos was converted. The chief cult of the city was that of the goddess Artemis or Diana, and her temple was one of the wonders of the ancient world. Fanatic devotion to this pagan deity occasioned the opposition to Paul's ministry here, but God enabled him to establish a strong church which became a headquarters for the evangelization of the entire province of Asia. Enthusiastic pagans became enthusiastic Christians, but by the time Christ wrote this brief epistle in Revelation 2, the Christians had lost their first love. This letter, from the One who holds the seven stars in his right hand and walks in the middle of the seven candlesticks, is an effort to win the church back to full fellowship. Here we see Christ as the great Preserver and Watchman exhorting the Ephesians to repent, or else "I (will) come to thee, and will move thy candlestick out of its place" (2:5).

Today the magnificent ruins of Ephesus lie near the modern town of Selchuk or Selcuk. The site is completely desolate and is a swampy area in rainy seasons. Malarial death brooded here until the city gradually moved to a higher site, and thus it literally "moved out of its place."

CHRIST'S MESSAGE TO SMYRNA (2:8-11)

Smyrna ("myrrh") was a wealthy, prosperous, and dissolute city of Ionia. It was located about forty miles north of

[3]/See Thomas Cosmades, "Ruins of the Seven Churches," *Christianity Today* (December 4, 1964), p. 16.

Ephesus. Smyrna was inhabited mostly by Jews bitterly opposed to Christianity, so the Christians here suffered much persecution. It was Polycarp's field of Christian service, and it was here that he suffered martyrdom at the hands of a Roman soldier about A.D. 169. The city of Smyrna was founded as a Greek colony about a thousand years before Christ. It was conquered by the Asiatic Lydians about 300 years later but regained its Greek characteristics in the third century B.C., when it became an ally of Rome. Smyrna has been under Turkish rule since about A.D. 1500 and is now the modern port city of Izmir. Modern Smyrna has a population of nearly half a million and is Turkey's third largest city.

Christ's description of himself to this church as "the First and the Last, who was dead and lived again" was especially fitting, since the city of Smyrna had virtually died under the Lydians, but lived again four hundred years later. So Christ as the firstfruits of the resurrection encouraged these persecuted Christians who were threatened with martyrdom. Christ commends the church at Smyrna on several points and apparently withholds any condemnation. But though this church grew strong under the adverse winds of persecution, today this largest modern city in the area of the seven churches contains hardly a single believer!

CHRIST'S MESSAGE TO PERGAMUM (2:12-17)

Pergamum (*púrgos,* a tower, plus *gámos,* marriage) was a city of Mysia in Asia Minor which was located about three miles north of the River Bakyrchai (the ancient Caicus) and about twenty miles from the Aegean Sea. Pergamum was the seat of the Roman supreme court and was a headquarters for the opposition of the gospel. The city was largely addicted to idolatry, and its many temples were devoted to sensuous worship—notice "where Satan's throne is"[4] and "where Satan dwelleth" (2:13). Pergamum was also the chief seat of the Imperial cult of Rome, which worshipped Ascelpius as the

---

4/J. Dwight Pentecost, *Prophecy for Today* (Grand Rapids: Zondervan Publishing House, 1961), p. 133, reference to Pergamum.

Savior. It had a library of 200,000 volumes, and it was here that the art of making parchment, called "pergamena," was discovered. Modern Pergamum is known as Bergama and is located near the ruins of the ancient city. Its population today is only about 20,000.

The description of Christ as the One carrying the sharp, two-edged sword was especially appropriate because it encouraged the Christians to meet the Roman authority with the power of Christ's Word, which could overcome the threats of politics and religion. Some of these Christians stood true even at the cost of their lives. Others, however, lapsed into the teaching of Balaam[5] and still others adopted the teaching of the Nicolaitans. Although both these heresies condoned immorality, some scholars believe that the etymology of the word "Nicolaitans" (*nikáō*, to conquer, plus *laós*, people) indicates an unscriptural separation of the church into "priests" and "laymen." The Nicolaitan church may therefore have incorporated an embryonic form of Romanism. The doctrine that Ephesus hated became rooted in Pergamum!

CHRIST'S MESSAGE TO THYATIRA (2:18-29)

Thyatira ("daughter"?) was a city of Asia Minor situated between Pergamum and Sardis and a little south of the river Hyllus. The modern Turkish city of Akhisar (White Castle, with a population of 30,000), now marks the site of the ancient city. The city had a high reputation for its scarlet dyes, and Luke mentions Lydia of Philippi as a seller of purple from Thyatira.[6]

However, the church of Thyatira became seduced by iniquity, fornication, and spiritual idolatry, and the guilds became a great snare to the church. The name "Thyatira" may be a combination of *thugátēr*, daughter, and *teírō*, to oppress, distress, weaken. If so, it conveys the idea of feminine oppression and a "Jezebel morality." Whether Jezebel[7] was an

---

5/Num. 22:1—25:9; 2 Pet. 2:15, 16.
6/Acts 16:14.
7/1 Kings 16:29-33

actual woman of Thyatira or simply a symbol of the city's spiritual condition, we cannot help but notice the intensification of evil from "those who hold the teaching" of Balaam and the Nicolaitans in Pergamum to the *official* teaching of idolatry and fornication in Thyatira. Through the centuries both the church of Thyatira and the commercial prominence of the city have vanished.

The description of Christ's eyes as a flame of fire and his feet like burnished brass shows the penetrating judgment necessary to deal with the gross idolatry, hidden sins, and Satanic seduction which was practiced in Thyatira.

We should note that the first mention in these seven letters of Christ's second coming appears in the exhortation "hold fast till I come" (2:25). (I believe that the "comings" of 2:5, 16 refer to local judgments of erring churches.) Note also that in the last four letters to the churches the sequence of the admonitions and promises is reversed, so that the promise to the overcomer precedes the admonition "He that hath an ear. . . ." These two phenomena suggest that the seven letters should be divided into groups of three and four. Another cue to this division is that while Christ addressed only one group in the first three churches, here in Thyatira he speaks to *two* groups—the faithful remnant who followed the teachings of Christ and the unfaithful religionists who followed the teachings of Jezebel.

In this first mention of his second coming (2:25-27), our Lord promises the overcomer that he will share Christ's rule over the nations.

CHRIST'S MESSAGE TO SARDIS (3:1-6)

Sardis ("remnant" or "escaped few"?) was a city of west Asia Minor about fifty miles east of Smyrna. It was the capital of Lydia and was noted for its manufacture of woolen goods and carpets. Wealthy citizens pursued mystery cults, and the church was upbraided for its sham Christianity. An earthquake overturned the city in A.D. 17, during the reign of Tiberias and before Revelation was written. This helps us to understand the exhortation to "strengthen the things which remain" (3:2, KJV). Today nothing remains but dirt, ancient mounds, and a poor village known as Sart. Ancient Sardis has become a dead city and a dead church, with the ruins of a heathen temple alongside the ruins of a Christian church.

The picture of Christ possessing the seven Spirits of God and holding seven stars emphasizes his perfect wisdom and complete sovereignty over his church. Even though the majority of the Sardis church was dying, Christ strengthened the small remnant that survived so that their names would not be blotted out of the book of life (3:5). Christ made no commendation because he found none of their works perfect before God. The lowest passing grade in God's school is 100%!

Here we find the second announcement of the coming of Christ, with the added exhortation to *watch,* since he will come as a thief.[8] Sardis represents a church with the reputation of sound theology but the experience of dead orthodoxy. However, the few overcomers among this group were promised a place before the Father and his angels.

CHRIST'S MESSAGE TO PHILADELPHIA (3:7-13)

Philadelphia, the "city of brotherly love," was located in Lydia of Asia Minor and had been built by Attalus Philadelphus. Its elevation was 952 feet above sea level. Philadelphia was a Roman town until A.D. 1392, when it fell into the hands of the Turks. In spite of several earthquakes, it still remains under the name of Alasehir (City of God) and carries on a flourishing trade with Smyrna. Its ancient walls still enclose a population of 12,000. Even though Philadelphia and Smyrna received no condemnation from Christ, they lost most of their testimony in subsequent centuries and bear no Christian witness at all today.

The characterization of Christ as the holy and true One with the key of David was especially fitting, since Philadelphia was the church of the open door of evangelism[9] and the open

---

8/Cf. Matt. 24:43, 44; Luke 12:39; 1 Thess. 5:2, 4; 2 Pet. 3:10; Rev. 16:15.
9/Acts 14:27.

door of escape.[10] The city lay directly on the imperial Roman road, and its long valley constituted an open door to Phrygia and the regions beyond. And Christ said that no one could shut his open door. Philadelphia was a missionary city from its inception, for it had been founded to spread the Hellenistic civilization eastward. But now the open door of the church was her new mission, a calling which no human power can ever destroy.

The third mention of Christ's second coming occurs in this letter, with the added information "I come quickly" (3: 11). Christ's reward for keeping the word of his patience would be to keep his people "from the hour of trial, that hour which is to come upon the whole world, to try them that dwell upon the earth" (3:10). So the One who has the key of David will also protect his overcomers from the woes of the Great Tribulation.[11]

The climactic way in which the second coming of Christ is presented to these last three churches—"I come" (the fact), "as a thief" (the manner), and "quickly" (the time)— implies strongly that these messages apply to various periods of church history down to the second coming of Christ.

CHRIST'S MESSAGE TO LAODICEA (3:14-22)

Laodicea (*laós,* people, plus *díkē,* judgment or justice) was located on the banks of the Lycus, within the confines of Phrygia and Lydia and about forty miles from Ephesus. Laodicea was once the capital of greater Phrygia but is now a heap of ruins called *Eski-hissar* or "old castle." The name "Laodicea" designates a church of mob rule, in which everything is swayed by clamor and voting rather than by the voice of the Holy Spirit.

The characterization of Christ as "the Amen, the faithful and true witness, the beginning of the creation of God" is drawn from the prologue of Revelation rather than from the description of Christ in the latter part of Chapter 1. Notice the

---

10/Rev. 3:10; 4:1; Luke 21:36; 1 Thess. 4:17; 5:9, 10.
11/Isa. 22:22.

ASV marginal reading of Isaiah 65:16, in which "the God of Amen" is an alternate for "the God of Truth." The serious condition of this lukewarm church, whose members thought they needed nothing, called for a re-emphasis on the truth as a principle and on the truth personified in Christ himself. As "the faithful and true witness" to the truth Christ challenged the church of Laodicea about her lukewarm condition. Verse 14 also serves as a summary statement for this whole section on the seven churches. The confirmation of this truth comes from Christ, who is also "the beginning of the creation of God"; he is "before all things, and in him all things consist" (Col. 1:17). Christ is the Creator who began all created things (John 1:3).

Since Christ is eternal, he judges Laodicea by his own eternal standards. Not only does he find nothing worthy of commendation, but this is the only church where Christ is seen standing "outside." He stands at the door and knocks, and his appeal is to individuals rather than to the whole—"If *any man* . . ." (3:20). There is no mention of Christ's second advent (unless "standing at the door" indicates that he has already come), but there is a call to repentance. Remember that the coming of Christ reached a climax in the previous church, and that the Philadelphians were promised escape from the hour of trial. What does all this mean? Are the Laodiceans left to go through the Great Tribulation? Have they missed the rapture?

OBSERVATIONS, INTERPRETATIONS, AND APPLICATION

To the Churches of Asia

Actual Congregations

These seven churches of Asia were actual congregations located in seven different cities of Asia Minor at the time of John's writing. All the conditions described in these letters actually prevailed at the end of the first century A.D.

Particular pastors

Each letter was addressed to the "angel" (pastor or messenger) of a particular congregation, and the conditions described in each letter represented the congregation as a whole.

To the Church Universal

Representative of John's day

The admonition "he that hath an ear" near the end of each letter was addressed to *all* the churches. So there were people in *every* church who needed *all seven* messages. This shows the necessity of seven different messages.

Since there were many churches in Asia Minor at the time of John's writing, these seven were selected by Christ because they represented the conditions of *all* the churches at that time. So these seven letters were addressed to all the churches then in existence.

Representative of church history

Since seven is the number of perfection or completeness, these messages include all of church history. Also, Jesus is seen "in the midst of" the seven golden candlesticks. Since Christ is in every true church, all churches of all ages are represented in these seven letters, including the church of our present day. Would it be fanciful to say that certain conditions were more characteristic of particular periods of church history than others? Is there a correlation between the successive eras of church history and the characteristics of the seven churches of Revelation? Here are some suggested correlations:

Ephesus—the church at the end of the first century, characteristic because she then left her first love.

Smyrna—the period of great persecutions, from the first century to A.D. 316. Myrrh signifies persecution.

Pergamum—the beginning of the church and state under Constantine, A.D. 316 to 500. The name "Pergamum" suggests elevation and marriage—the church elevated to the throne and married to the state.[12]

Thyatira—the result of the marriage of the church and the

12/See Pentecost, *op. cit.*, for the act of Constantine which brought Babylonianism into the church.

state, producing the "daughter," Romanism, and bringing in the dark ages, A.D. 500 to 1500.

Sardis—the period of the Reformation under Luther, Cran-
mer, Knox, Doddridge, Baxter, and the Wesleys, A.D.
1500 to 1900. The name "Sardis" suggests a "remnant."

Philadelphia—the church of "brotherly love" and of the
"open door" of opportunity for worldwide evangelism
and of escape from the Great Tribulation. Could this be
the twentieth-century church?

Laodicea—the dead, formal, democratic, apostate church
that is left to go through the Great Tribulation.

To the Church of Our Day

The existence of seven types

Our observations of these seven churches up to this point
show both a historical sequence and a contemporary rele-
vance. This implies that we live in the Philadelphian age
rather than the Laodicean period. This does not mean that
some of the other church conditions are nonexistent today,
for all seven groups of characteristics have existed from the
first century until now. What the implication does mean is
that we are now living during the church's greatest era of
gospel opportunity. Later we will give other reasons for reaching
this conclusion.

The emphasis on one type

Even though all seven types of churches exist in our day,
the primary emphasis is on one type—the Philadelphian
church. Though Christ's coming is not mentioned in the letters
to the first three churches, it is mentioned in each of the next
three. To Thyatira Christ said, "That which ye have, hold
fast *till I come*" (2:25). To Sardis he said, "If therefore thou
shalt not watch, *I will come as a thief,* and thou shalt not
know what hour I will come upon thee" (3:3). To Philadelphia he said, *"I come quickly;* hold fast that which thou hast,
that no one take thy crown" (3:11). So the *fact* of Christ's
coming is announced to Thyatira, the *uncertainty of the time*
is emphasized to Sardis, and the *imminence* of Christ's coming
is the new element in Philadelphia.

Philadelphia is given the only promise of escape from the worldwide hour of trial. "Because thou didst keep the word of my patience, I also will keep thee from the hour of trial, that hour which is to come upon the whole world, to try them that dwell upon the earth."[13] These "earth-dwellers" are in contrast to God's people, who as pilgrims and strangers "tabernacle" (*skēnóō*, dwell temporarily) on earth while they wait expectantly for their heavenly home. So the imminence of Christ's coming and the promise of escape from the Great Tribulation appear in the same church. Does this not imply that both these events will be realized during the Philadelphian age? And are we not living in this period right now?

Significantly, the coming of Christ is never mentioned in the letter to Laodicea, and this is the only letter in which Christ stands outside, knocking and appealing to the *individual* for entrance—"If *any man* hear my voice and open the door, I will come in to *him,* and will sup with *him,* and *he* with me" (3:20). He came for the Philadelphians, but the Laodiceans were left behind. Why? Because they were lukewarm. But Christ has not forsaken them entirely; he still stands at the door to give individuals a chance to be saved—even during the Great Tribulation.

Certainly the true church today is not all that she should be, but she has "a little power," she is keeping God's Word, and she has not denied Christ's name (3:8). There are many Laodiceans and there is much lukewarmness, but Christ is not dealing with this spurious element; he is dealing with the true church—the Philadelphians—and he is not outside the door. He is still in our midst! Hallelujah!

To the Individual of Our Day

The current belief that we are in the Laodicean period is one of the greatest hindrances to revival today. God reminded Elijah that there were seven thousand people who had not

---

13/Rev. 3:10. The word for "dwell" here is *katoikéō,* meaning "to dwell, settle down"; not *skēnóō,* meaning "to tent, dwell temporarily, tabernacle," as in John 1:14. Compare G. H. Lang, *The Histories and Prophecies of Daniel* (London: The Paternoster Press, 1950), p. 195.

bowed their knees to Baal. Let him remind you that we are living in the age of evangelism. This is the most successful missionary period that the world has ever known, and the mustard tree of Matthew 13:31, 32 has literally filled the earth. In spite of widespread apostasy, God has promised to send a gracious outpouring of his Spirit at the end of this age,[14] even as he did at Pentecost. It will be "as the latter and former rain unto the earth," and he is looking for cooperative intercessors in order to bring this to pass. May he count on you and me?

---

[14]/Joel 2:28-32.

PART THREE

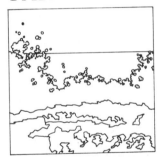

CHRIST
IN THE CONFLICT

5

CHRIST PREPARES FOR THE CONFLICT

Revelation 4, 5

INSTRUCTIONS FOR STUDYING REVELATION 4 AND 5

First read Luke 21:24-38 as your devotional approach to this section, praying that you may be accounted worthy to escape. Then study Revelation 4 and 5, using all the study techniques you have learned so far. Be sure that the additions to your chart are Christ-centered, for this book is a Revelation of *Jesus Christ*. As you try to determine the order of events, do not lose sight of the worthy Savior. Don't argue with people who disagree with you, and don't be too surprised when you find that godly scholars disagree with each other. Be charitable to all and pray for the illumination of the Holy Spirit. Be willing to exchange old views for new ones if they are clearly taught in the Book. Above all, favor interpretations which demand holy living rather than loose living. Shun any interpretations which delay our Lord from coming this very hour.

The following questions are designed to help you in your independent study, but do not limit your study to answering a list of questions. This is *not* intended as a "question-and-answer" Bible study!

1. What is the change of viewpoint in Revelation 4 and 5?

2. What is the significance of "Come up hither" in 4:1? To whom are these words spoken?
3. Who do the twenty-four elders represent?
4. Who do the living creatures represent?
5. What is the seven-sealed scroll? Who is found worthy to open it?
6. Why could not the Father open it?
7. Can you envision the central throne and everything surrounding it? Though the descriptions of the throne are intended to give us some idea of its grandeur, remember that *relationships* are more important than *geometric layout.*
8. Who are the persons connected with the throne? Can you find the Trinity?

Learn to read as an artist interprets. Now read Revelation 5 as a musician would, singing along with the twenty-four elders. Worship the Lamb who is worthy and join in with the universal adoration of the Lamb who is King!

Do not read the rest of this chapter until you have done your independent study. This part of Revelation is the most majestic and overwhelming portion of Scripture up to this point!

NOTES ON REVELATION 4, 5

THE RAPTURE OF JOHN (4:1)

The Christ who was central in the churches in Revelation 2 and 3 is now preparing for the conflict of the Great Tribulation in Chapters 4 and 5. The opening words of Revelation 4 introduce a complete change of perspective. John is transported from earth to heaven, from the present to the future, and from the first vision to the second. The transfer from earth to heaven is indicated by the trumpet-like voice of Christ saying to John, "Come up hither" (4:1). At this time John, like Enoch and Elijah of old, has the rare privilege of being translated from earth to heaven. But John's experience far exceeds that of the Old Testament saints, for he is to have a firsthand preview of future events from the beginning of the Great Tribulation to the beginning of the eternal ages.

The transfer from the present to the future is indicated by two expressions: "After these things" and "I will show thee the things which must come to pass hereafter" (4:1). The transfer from the first vision to the second is indicated by the second occurrence of the key sentence: "I was in the Spirit" (4:2). This new section of the apocalyptic panorama takes us to the end of Chapter 16, and it presents Christ in the conflict. In this section we will notice the prominence of the throne in heaven and the centrality of Christ as the slain Lamb throughout the whole scene of action.

In Revelation 4:1 John's attention is called to an opened door in heaven. Formerly this was a door of evangelism or exit (3:8), but now it is the door of entrance into heaven. This door of escape enables John to enter heaven before the awful judgments of the Great Tribulation begin (6:2). His response to the invitation "Come up hither" may be identified with the snatching away of the saints in 1 Thessalonians 4: 13-18 and 1 Corinthians 15:51-57. John seems to have been simultaneously "caught up hither" and "in the Spirit."

THE THRONE IN HEAVEN (4:2-11)

The Enthroned Father (4:2, 3)

The word "throne" (*thrónos*) occurs forty-six times in Revelation, and fourteen of these occurrences are in Chapter 4. The center of interest, however, is not the throne itself but on the Person sitting on the throne (4:2). He is none other than God the Father. Though John attempts the impossible in describing this Personage, he manages to convey certain concepts to us by likening him to the brilliance of a diamond and the glowing radiance of a carnelian. The entire description pictures majesty joined to judgment, with the translucent green rainbow of promise in the background.[1]

1/Cf. Dan. 7:9-13.

The Twenty-Four Elders (4:4)

Surrounding this central throne of awful majesty are twenty-four lesser thrones, but again the center of interest is not the thrones themselves but the elders on these thrones. Who are these elders? Some think they are heavenly beings, but since the word *presbúteros* (elder) is used in Scripture only of human beings, the "elders" could be neither angels nor heavenly spirits. An overwhelming majority of commentators agree that they are glorified human beings.[2] In other words, they are seniors of the celestial assembly and firstfruits of the rapture. These honored officials are the firstborn of the household, and they probably include John himself, since the elders represent not only the twelve tribes of Israel but also the twelve apostles. God has made them to be both priests and "a kingdom" unto the Father (1:6; 5:9).

There are four more reasons for identifying the elders as human beings who have entered into their eternal reward. First, since everything that follows Revelation 4:1 refers to the future, the elders could hardly represent the present life of Christian victory. Second, they have already received their crowns and thrones (2:10, 26, 27). Third, the number twenty-four is double the symbolic number of government. This double government probably consists of the twelve tribes of Israel and the twelve apostles (representing the New Testament saints). Jesus said, "Many shall come from the east and the west, and shall sit down with Abraham and Isaac and Jacob in the kingdom of heaven."[3] So both Old and New Testament saints will have a part in this kingdom. The enthroned elders are not central in the picture, and their power is only delegated. Their true source of power is the Personage on the central throne—God the Father. Finally, the elders must be redeemed human beings because they sing a new song of redemption (5:9).

2/Alford, Barnes, Benson, Binney, Carpenter, Clarke, Clemance, Cook, Crafer, Crosby, Dusterdieck, Fausset, Girdlestone, Godet, Gray, Hengstenberg, Henry, Holden, Kuyper, Milligan, Plummer, Robertson, Scott, Sheppard, Simcox, Slight, Smith, Swete, Vincent, Weidner.
3/Matt. 8:11. See page 182 and Rev. 18:20; 21:12, 14.

The Sevenfold Holy Spirit (4:5)

As in Revelation 1:4, the seven Spirits of God represent the perfection of the Holy Spirit as he works throughout the world.[4] The seven torches of fire remind us of the work which he began at Pentecost—that of equipping men to carry the torch of the gospel into all the world. The transparent (not "glassy") sea symbolizes the fact that everything is clear to the Spirit, who reveals the deep things of God to his saints.

The Four Living Creatures (4:6-11)

The four living creatures (*zōón*) are not to be confused with the wild beasts (*thēríon*) of Revelation 13. Nor does their name allow the interpretation that they are angels, for angels are never symbolized in Revelation. Also, the living creatures appear side by side with angels (5:11). It is true that these living creatures have their counterpart in the Old Testament,[5] but these Old Testament passages do not govern the interpretation of Revelation.

It has been said that Revelation contains 278 quotations of the Old Testament in 404 verses, but close scrutiny shows that most of these are adaptations rather than true quotations. These adaptations of Old Testament rituals are especially effective in portraying the glories of heaven.

But exactly who are the "living creatures"? "They are redeemed men, glorified and related to the judgment-throne in heaven and to the interests and affairs of the future kingdom on earth, as the cherubim are related to the throne and kingdom now and in the former dispensations."[6] The living creatures represent the agents of the universal rule of the throne of God. Their six wings signify swiftness for carrying out God's will, and their many eyes give perfect vision in the execution of the new order. The significance of their four faces may be shown as follows:

---

[4]/Three is the number of the trinity of God, and four is the number of the world. The combination, which makes seven, often indicates the acts of God worldward.

[5]/Gen. 3:24; Isa. 6:2; Ezek. 1:4-28; 10:1-22.

[6]/Seiss, *op. cit.*, p. 107.

Lion—responsibility for the wild places of the earth.

Young bull—responsibility for the cultivated places of the earth.

Human countenance—responsibility for the cities, towns, and villages.

Flying eagle—responsibility for the whole expanse of air and sky.[7]

So the living creatures represent the agents of the universal rule of the throne of God. The difference between the work of the elders and the living creatures may be compared as follows:

The *elders* are the agents of God's Word, and they represent the worship of redeemed man. They are the counsellors.

The *living creatures* are the agents of God's providence, and they represent the service of redeemed man. They are the executors.[8]

The Tersanctus ("holy, holy, holy") of Revelation 4 shows worship directed to the Father as Creator (4:8, 11). In Chapter 5 the worship is directed to the Lamb because he is the Redeemer (5:9).

THE SEVEN-SEALED BOOK (5:1-8)

The vision of Revelation 4 centered around the enthroned Father, but in Chapter 5 the emphasis is on the slain Lamb. How is he introduced? The Father has on his right hand a book filled with writing, but it is tightly sealed with seven seals. Even though the Father is offering this book by holding it on his open palm, no one seems worthy to grasp and open it. After a futile search throughout heaven and earth for a worthy personage, John breaks out into copious weeping. Then one of the elders comforts him with these words: "Weep not; behold, the Lion that is of the tribe of Judah, the Root of David,[9]

7/Lenski, *op. cit.,* p. 183.
8/Cf. Rev. 15:7.
9/Cf. Gen. 49:9, 10; Isa. 11:1, 10; Luke 1:32, 33; Rom. 15:12; Rev. 22:16.

hath overcome to open the book and the seven seals thereof"
(5:5).

The number seven here has the same significance as in
other contexts; it shows the acts of God upon the world. In
other words, it is necessary to purge the world with the awful
judgments contained in the scroll in order to dispossess the
usurper, Satan,[10] and to set up the kingdom of heaven on
earth. Thus an appropriate title for this book is *The Title
Deed to the Earth.* This was the title deed that had originally
been given to Adam but was reclaimed by God after the fall
of man.[11]

Christ is represented here as the unique Conqueror because of the tremendous victory which he won on the Cross.
Now any opposition from men or demons only serves to en-
hance and display Christ's victory. He is represented not
merely as a Conqueror but as possessing seven horns of perfect
power, seven eyes of perfect perspective, and seven Spirits of
God[12] sent forth into all the earth. Now this same perfection
will be directed to the worldwide tribulation judgments, for
Christ himself is preparing for the conflict. The taking of the
title deed by the slain Lamb is the crux of the book.

THE WORSHIPPING MYRIADS (5:9-14)

When Christ comes to the outstretched hand of the Father
and takes the book, the four living creatures and twenty-four
elders fall down before him in worship. Their bowls filled
with incense show that the saints' prayers during millenniums
past are now being answered, and their new song exalts the
Christ who redeemed them and made them a kingdom and
priests unto God.

All creation—living creatures, elders, and angels—now
joins in ascribing to the Father and Son eternal blessing, honor,
glory, and dominion. The four living creatures keep saying
"Amen" and the elders fall down in worship. Though Handel's

10/Satan is called the god of this world in 2 Cor. 4:4.
11/Gen. 1:26.
12/Since the seven eyes of the Lamb represent the Holy Spirit, we should
recognize the presence of the Spirit each time the Lamb is mentioned.

Messiah gives some idea of the grandeur and majesty of this moment, God's full glory is totally beyond our human imagination. Heaven is not a world of ethereal mists and shadows, but of beautiful substance and realities!

SUMMARY

We have seen that everything following Revelation 4:1 occurs at the end of the church age. Because the Philadelphians are promised escape from the Great Tribulation, we noted that John represents the rapture of the overcomers. These overcomers are also represented by the elders and the living creatures.

Everything in heaven centers around the enthroned Father, the sevenfold Holy Spirit, and the slain Lamb. The twenty-four thrones of the elders and four living creatures surround that one central throne, and all these saints join the hosts of angels in heaven's ultimate paean of praise: "Worthy is the Lamb that hath been slain to receive the power, and riches, and wisdom, and might, and honor, and glory, and blessing . . . Unto him that sitteth on the throne, and unto the Lamb, be the blessing, and the honor, and the glory, and the dominion, for ever and ever" (5:12, 13).

THE SEVEN KEYS TO REVELATION

John's Emphasis on Christ

The most important key to Revelation is John's emphasis on Christ. This emphasis is found in the title (The Revelation of Jesus Christ), the theme (The Personal and Universal Coming of Christ), and the signature (The Eternal, Almighty Son). The Prologue (1:1-8) and Epilogue (22:6-21) each contain five announcements of the coming of Christ.

The key phrase "in the Spirit" indicates the biographical or Christological divisions of the book and occurs in Revelation 1:10, 4:2, 17:3, and 21:10. The first "in-Spirit" showing occurs on a certain Sunday in A.D. 95 on the Isle of Patmos and presents *Christ in the churches* (1:9—3:22). This presentation describes Christ the Living One and Christ the Promising One, and it includes his message to the seven churches.

The second showing presents *Christ in the conflict* (4:1—16:21). Here we see Christ the Worthy One, Christ the Judging One, Christ the Delivering One, and Christ the Holy One. This presentation includes the seven seals, the seven trumpets, the seven personages, and the seven bowls.

The third showing presents *Christ in the conquest* (17:1 —20:15). This great showing contains the climax of the book and presents Christ the Reigning One. It includes the seven dooms and takes the viewer up to the threshold of the eternal ages.

The fourth showing presents *Christ in the Consummation* (21:1—22:5). The key sentence does not occur until 21:10, but the eternal ages begin with the new heaven and the new earth in the first part of the chapter. This showing presents Christ the Comforting One, and it includes the seven "new things."

In the prologue we see *Christ corresponding* and in the epilogue *Christ calling*. Both present him as the Coming One.

John's Inspired Chronology

The key verses (1:19, 20) contain the chronological outline of the book: "Write therefore a) the things which thou sawest (*ha eídes,* second aorist indicative, indicating the past and including Chapter 1), and b) the things which are (*ha eisín,* present indicative, indicating the present church age and including Chapters 2 and 3), and c) the things which shall come to pass hereafter (*ha méllei genésthai metà taúta,* indicating the imminent future and including Chapters 4—22).

John's Inspired Symbolism

The key verses also show that Revelation must be interpreted symbolically in those passages where literal interpretation is not possible. Here the word "mystery" (*mustérion*), one of the three key words, shows that the seven stars are seven messengers or pastors of the seven churches. The word "mystery" does not indicate something that cannot be understood, but something that requires revelation. It denotes a secret which requires supernatural disclosure. The other mysteries in Revelation are the announcing of the consummation (10: 7), Mystery Babylon the Great (17:5), and the mystery of the woman (17:7).

The second key word which indicates symbolism is "sign" (*sēmeíon*) and "to signify" (*sēmaínō*). The verb means "to make known by signs and symbols," and it occurs only in Revelation 1:1. The noun occurs seven times as follows: (1) the sign of the woman in 12:1, (2) the sign of the red dragon in 12:3, (3) the great signs performed by the second beast of 13:13, 14 and 19:20, (4) the sign of the seven plagues or bowls of 15:1 and 16:14.

The third key word which indicates symbolism is "wonder" (*thaúma*), "to wonder" (*thaumázō*), and "wonderful" (*thaumastós*). The verb form is found in 13:3, where the whole earth wondered after the beast, and in 17:6, 7, 8, where John and the earth-dwellers wondered at the sight of the drunken harlot. The adjective form is found in 15:1, 3, where it describes the sign of the seven angels with the seven plagues or bowls as part of the marvelous works of God. The noun form occurs in 17:6, where the drunken harlot is described as a great wonder.

John's Overlapping Chronology

As in the Book of Daniel, where Chapters 5 and 7 run parallel in time (as well as Chapters 6 and 9), the chronology of the Revelation overlaps in places. This should not seem strange to us, since many secular classics of literature are written in the same way. It is often impossible to tell a story or relate the events of history without using this overlapping plan, especially when the principal characters are in different locations while important events are occurring simultaneously. In Revelation simultaneous events in heaven, on earth, and under the earth are described in separate passages. The ribbon chart on page 78 will help you identify the chronology of these events.

John's Use of the Law of Recurrence

The law of recurrence is "that peculiarity of the Holy Spirit . . . by which he gives first the outlines of a subject, then recurs to it again for the purpose of adding details."[13] Many people have overlooked this principle of interpretation, and the result has been confusion and misunderstanding. This principle is illustrated in the complementary creation accounts of Genesis 1 and 2. Genesis 1 describes the creation of the universe, the world, and the inhabitants of the world while Chapter 2 provides further details of the creation of man.[14]

In Revelation the law of recurrence occurs for the first time in Chapters 1 through 3. The churches are mentioned in Chapter 1 but are fully discussed only in Chapters 2 and 3.

STUDY PROJECT NUMBER 5

How many other illustrations of the law of recurrence can you find in Revelation? Begin your list now and watch it grow as you proceed. It will solve many problems of interpretation for you.

John's Vision of the Thrones

Chapters 4 and 5 form a single, continuous passage which contains the setting or "backdrop" for the rest of the book. Keep in mind that whenever the throne is mentioned, the stated or implied emphasis is always on the Trinity as the ruling Godhead. After the enthroned Father, the sevenfold Holy Spirit, and the slain Lamb are thoroughly described, there is no need to repeat all three names each time. In some passages the word "throne" itself represents the presence of the entire Godhead.

The Way to the Throne

John found his way to the throne through the open door of

13/James M. Gray, *Synthetic Bible Studies* (New York: Fleming H. Revell Company, 1923), p. 12.
14/Joseph P. Free, *Archaeology and Bible History* (Wheaton: Van Kampen Press, 1950), p. 15.

the rapture. John's glorious preview experience identifies him with the twenty-four elders and the four living creatures. These enthroned elders have already received their rewards and are ruling and reigning with Christ (2:26, 27). Since all these events are actually still in the future, John enjoyed the unique privilege of previewing the very glories of heaven!

The Book from the Throne

The seven-sealed book or scroll of tribulation judgments is the title deed to the earth. It had been given to Adam but was repossessed by God after the fall of man. Now the earth must be cleansed for the reign of Christ, and only the slain Lamb is worthy to perform this task and rid the world of the usurper, Satan.

The Worship at the Throne

Worship rises to a new peak at this point. The praise is based not simply on creation but also on redemption. The doxologies of Revelation 4:11 and 5:9, 11, 13 incorporate choirs of ever-increasing numbers, until at last all creation joins in ascribing blessing, honor, glory, and dominion to the Father and the Son. The Holy Spirit makes all this possible through the perfect illumination of the seven torches of fire before the throne.

The Recurrence of the Throne

Ten chapters in Revelation connect major events with the throne. Four events are related to judgment, three to rapture, and three to the eternal ages. The first event is the response of earth-dwellers to the opening of the sixth seal judgment. Because of the fearful earthquake, they say to the mountains and the rocks, "Fall on us, and hide us from the face of him that sitteth on the *throne,* and from the wrath of the Lamb" (6:16).

The second event is the worship by the great multitude of Gentiles who have been translated out of the middle of the Great Tribulation. Their worship is directed to "God, who sitteth on the *throne,* and unto the Lamb" (7:10).

The third event is another judgment scene prior to the series of trumpets. An angel stands over the golden altar with a golden censer, adding incense to the prayers of the saints on the altar before the *throne* (8:3).

The fourth event is the rapture of the man-child, "who is to rule all the nations with a rod of iron; and her child was caught up to God, and unto his *throne*" (12:5; cf. 2:26, 27).

The fifth event is the rapture of the 144,000 Jews, who now sing "a new song before the *throne*" because they have been "purchased out of the earth" (14:3).

The sixth event is the solemn announcement of the seventh bowl judgment by "a great voice out of the temple from the *throne,* saying, It is done" (16:17).

The seventh event is the judging of the wicked dead before the "great white *throne,* and him that sat upon it, from whose face the earth and the heaven fled away; and there was found no place for them" (20:11).

The eighth event is the making of all things new for the beginning of the eternal ages. "And he that sitteth on the *throne* said, Behold, I make all things new" (21:5).

The ninth event is the showing of "a river of water of life, bright as crystal, proceeding out of the *throne* of God and of the Lamb, in the midst of the street" of the paradise of God (22:1).

The tenth event is the removal of the curse introduced by the fall of man. "And there shall be no curse anymore; and the *throne* of God and of the Lamb shall be therein; and his servants shall serve him, and they shall see his face, and his name shall be on their foreheads" (22:3, 4). Praise God!

John's Participation in the Future

The seventh key to the understanding of Revelation is John's participation in the future. We have already seen that John's rapture in Chapter 4 identifies him with the elders and the living creatures. But in Revelation 10:9 John is asked to eat the open book held by the angel who stands on the earth and sea. We will say more about this when we study Revelation 10. In Revelation 11:1 John continues his role as a par-

CHRONOLOGICAL RIBBON CHART OF REVELATION

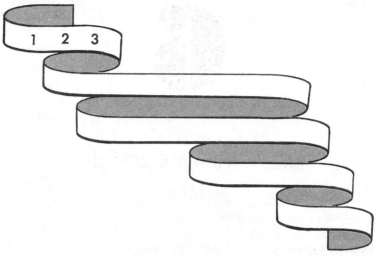

ticipant and not simply a spectator by rising and measuring the temple of God and the altar, "and them that worship therein." John does all this in response to specific commands from heaven.

John's emphasis on Christ, his inspired chronology, his inspired symbolism, his overlapping chronology, his use of the law of recurrence, his vision of the thrones, and his participation in the future are seven crucial keys to a thorough understanding of Revelation. See if you can discover even more keys to the meaning of the book!

John's overlapping chronology, discussed on page 74, may be illustrated on the above chart by placing the chapter numbers from 4 through 22 on the folds of this ribbon chart. The student should add these chapter numbers as the chronology of the book becomes clear to him through his own independent study.

CHRIST OPENS THE CONFLICT

Revelation 6

INSTRUCTIONS FOR STUDYING REVELATION 6

Read Matthew 24:15-31 as a devotional approach to this chapter. The eagles or vultures in Matthew 24:28 symbolize death and judgment during the Great Tribulation. Compare this event with the "supper of the great God" in Revelation 19:17. Now begin your independent study of Revelation 6, using all the study suggestions we have made so far. Are you tempted to omit some of the steps? *Don't.* Thank God for this opportunity to really dig deep! Use the following questions to stimulate your research.

1. When do the judgments in Chapter 6 take place? Relate them to the previous lesson, and then to the book as a whole.
2. Who is the rider on the white horse? Don't be deceived! Remember that the seals are *judgments*.
3. Do these seals follow in chronological order? Do they follow in *logical* order? Explain your answers.
4. Can you group the seals? Is there a division in the grouping? What are the indications for such a division?
5. What is the source of all these judgments?

6. Is each judgment separate, or do they all move toward a climax?
7. What is the purpose of these judgments?
8. How does the fourth seal differ from the preceding ones?
9. When were the souls under the altar slain? Why?
10. What do the white robes suggest? What are these souls waiting for?
11. Name the seven classes of men that will be affected by the opening of the sixth seal. What is significant about the mention of seven groups?
12. Why is there an interruption in the record between the sixth and seventh seals?

NOTES ON REVELATION 6

THE GREAT TRIBULATION

The Christ who walked among the churches in Revelation 2 and 3 and prepared for the conflict in Chapters 4 and 5 now opens the conflict in Chapter 6. When the slain Lamb took earth's title deed from the hand of the enthroned Father in Revelation 5, he was preparing to open the conflict of earth's final judgments. All these judgments were sealed in Christ's "title deed" or seven-sealed book. From the opening of the first seal in Revelation 6 to the pouring of the seventh bowl in Chapter 16, we see *Christ in the conflict.* This is the period which we call the Great Tribulation, and this great conflict engages all the forces of God and Satan.

Although the Old Testament prophets neither saw nor prophesied the church age, they did give a preview of the Great Tribulation. Jeremiah called it "the time of Jacob's trouble" (30:7) and Isaiah called it "the indignation" (26:20). Daniel called it "a time of trouble, such as never was since there was a nation even to that same time" (12:1). All three of these prophets envisioned final deliverance and salvation. Matthew calls it the "great tribulation, such as hath not been from the beginning of the world until now, no, nor ever shall be" (24:21; cf. vv. 22-28). Because Christ's prophetic discourse in Matthew 24, Mark 13, and Luke 21 has a Jewish tone and was spoken before the church was born at Pentecost, there is no mention of the rapture. Paul gives us the first clear teaching on the rapture in 1 Thessalonians 4. However, Revelation is the only book of the Bible that provides a full panorama of these future events. Although the rapture is not specifically mentioned in Revelation 4, it is strongly implied[1] by the presence of the elders and the living creatures and by the transfer of John from earth to heaven.[2] The Great Tribulation, which begins in Revelation 6, follows this transfer or rapture in Chapters 4 and 5; and Revelation 6 should therefore be interpreted in the light of the two preceding chapters. The judgments proceed from the enthroned saints and are spearheaded by Christ, the slain Lamb.

THE WHITE HORSE (6:1, 2)

The Great Tribulation begins with the appearance of four horses and their riders. When the Lamb opens the first seal, one of the living creatures thunders "Come" (*érchou*). This is a present imperative, signifying continuous action under the sovereign control of the Lamb. The words "and see" (as in KJV) are probably not part of the original Greek text. The summons is therefore not to John the spectator but to the white horse and his rider.

Who is the rider? Some say he is Christ, but Christ is the One who opens the seals. It is too early for his return as King of kings and Lord of lords (19:11-16), for this would place the Battle of Armageddon at the beginning of the Great Tribulation rather than at the end. This interpretation would make Christ a tool of judgment rather than the Judge himself. This view does not fit in with the identity of the other three horsemen whose sphere of activity is earthbound, and it does not harmonize with other scriptural descriptions of Christ with his bride in the air or in the heavenlies.

---

[1]/This would be classified as an ideological implication, such as the existence of God. See page 49, last paragraph.

[2]/See page 66.

A second interpretation makes the white horse rider the Holy Spirit. However, all the seals are judgments, while the Holy Spirit is a blessing. Also, the rider has delegated authority, suggested by verse 2: "there was *given* unto him a crown." The Holy Spirit, on the other hand, is never crowned. Then too, the Holy Spirit came at Pentecost, so his coming here at the beginning of the Great Tribulation would be rather late!

A third interpretation makes the first horseman the personification of Christianity, or perhaps moral conquest under the arrow of truth. But this moral conquest also began at Pentecost. Also, this interpretation does not synchronize with the picture of judgment represented by the other three horsemen and the other six seals.

A more satisfactory interpretation is that the white horse and his rider symbolize the appearance of the Antichrist. This view coincides with the prophecies of Daniel,[3] Christ,[4] and Paul.[5] The Prince of Daniel 9 makes a firm covenant with many for one week—the seven years of the Great Tribulation. He then breaks this covenant in the middle of the week, causes the sacrifice and the oblation to cease, and turns on the Jews in fierce persecution. So we may expect the last half of the Great Tribulation to be the worst.

Long before Revelation was written Paul comforted the Thessalonians with the hope of the rapture in 1 Thessalonians 4. In his second letter to these saints he assured them they had not missed the rapture, since the Antichrist had not yet been revealed (2 Thess. 2:1-12). And he could not be revealed, according to Paul, as long as the "restrainer" was present.

Who, then, is the restrainer? The restrainer is mentioned

---

[3]/The Antichrist is called the little horn of the fourth beast in Dan. 7, the little horn of the fourth horn of the he-goat in Dan. 8, the prince who destroys the city and sanctuary and breaks the covenant in Dan. 9, and the willful king in Dan. 11.

[4]/The Antichrist is called "the abomination of desolation" (Matt. 24:15; Mark 13:14), and the use of the personal pronoun "he" shows him to be more than an influence. He is a person.

[5]/The Antichrist is called "the man of sin," "the son of perdition," "he that opposeth and exalteth himself against all that is called God or that is worshipped," and the one who sets "himself forth as God" by Paul in 2 Thess. 2:3, 4.

in two different grammatical constructions. The first is "that which restraineth"[6] and the second is "he who restrains."[7] "He who restrains" can easily be identified with the Holy Spirit, the One who at this present day is restraining the revelation of the Antichrist. "That which restraineth" is a construction which is not used in English but is commonly used in New Testament Greek. The language often used the neuter singular to refer to a group of people. A good illustration is found in John 6:37—"All that which (neuter singular) the Father giveth me shall come unto me; and him (masculine singular) that cometh to me I will in no wise cast out." Here the neuter singular includes all who will ever be saved, and the Greek construction groups them as one neuter mass. But in the personal experience of salvation, "him" shows that each person must come individually. While predestination includes the whole mass of people who will be saved, each individual must make his calling and election sure[8] by actually coming to Christ through the exercise of his own free will. This Greek idiom shows that the phrase "that which" of 2 Thessalonians refers to the church, the only group of people that could restrain evil and the evil one.

This leads to the conclusion that the restrainer should be thought of as *the Church indwelt by the Holy Spirit*. Note that the rapture of the saints (4:1) takes place before the revelation of the Antichrist (6:1, 2). This removal of the restrainer does not mean that the Holy Spirit is totally absent from the world during the Great Tribulation, for that would make it impossible for anyone at all to be saved during this period. The Holy Spirit was, is, and always will be omnipresent, for he is God. What is the difference, then, between the relationship of the Holy Spirit to men during the church age and during the Great Tribulation? Possibly the same relationship will exist during the Great Tribulation as existed throughout the Old Testament. Remember that the Holy Spirit came at Pentecost primarily to form the body of Christ, his church. When the church is translated to heaven, this particular rela-

---

[6]/*Tó katéchon,* neuter singular, 2 Thess. 2:6. See page 114.
[7]/*Ho katéchon,* masculine singular, 2 Thess. 2:7.
[8]/2 Pet. 1:10.

tionship will no longer exist. The primary purpose of the Great Tribulation is the salvation of the Jews and their preparation for the millennial age. But God in his mercy will also save multitudes of Gentiles (7:9). Just as the Gospels and Acts provide the transition from Judaism to Christianity, so the Revelation describes the transition from Christianity to Israel, the Millennium, and eternity.

THE RED HORSE (6:3, 4)

When the Lamb opens the second seal, the second living creature gives the summons "Come." This time a red horse comes forth, and his rider takes peace from the earth. This second seal, which indicates war, is the result of the first, so the judgments are cumulative. Again the rider has *delegated* authority, for "there was *given* unto him a great sword." This is no ordinary sword. War, public executions, and killings will be beyond description. A preview of this condition is the present brutal treatment of evangelicals by Communists. What will it be during the Tribulation, when most of the "salt of the earth"[9] has been taken away?

THE BLACK HORSE (6:5, 6)

When the Lamb opens the third seal, the summons of the third living creature brings forth a black horse whose rider carries a balance scale. This scale is used to weigh wheat and barley, food for the common man. So with the Antichrist comes not only war but famine.[10] During this time of famine the most ordinary food will be weighed carefully and sold at exorbitant prices. A whole day's pay will buy only enough for one man! The words "hurt not the oil and the wine" mean either that these luxuries are beyond the reach of the ordinary purchaser or that they are plentiful but unable to adequately nourish the people.

9/Matt. 5:13.
10/Lam. 4:9; 5:10; Jer. 14:1, 2.

THE PALE HORSE (6:7, 8)

While the first three judgments are taking place, the Lamb opens the fourth seal. The fourth living creature summons a fourth horse and his rider. This horse is a pale green, something like the color of a corpse. His rider is death, and hades[11] follows him. He too has delegated power, and this power is exercised over the earth by killing one-fourth of the earth's population by sword, famine, pestilence, and wild animals.

THE TRIBULATION MARTYRS (6:9-11)

The fifth seal begins a new phase of judgment by revealing the souls under the altar, those tribulation martyrs who had been slain for the Word of God and for the testimony which they held. The seven seals should be divided into two groups of four and three for the following reasons:

1. The first four seals are called horsemen.
2. These horsemen are summoned by the four living creatures, but there is no summons for the last three seals.
3. The first four seals emphasize processes, but the last three emphasize results.

All seven seals, however, form a single pattern because of their cumulative effect. Here in the fifth seal the saints are martyred as a direct result of the activity of the four horsemen. The good have always suffered along with the bad, but since there is no summons we can say that the martyrdom of these saints comes as the permissive will of God rather than his directive will. But death does not end all for them, for their prayer to the Master indicates coming judgment by Christ, who will avenge the blood of his martyrs. The answer which they receive under the symbol of white robes indicates the sure hope of resurrection (7:13).

---

[11]/On death and hades see William R. Newell, *The Book of the Revelation* (Chicago: Moody Press, 1935), pp. 105, 106.

THE GREAT EARTHQUAKE (6:12-17)

When the Lamb opens the sixth seal, a great earthquake follows, producing terrifying changes in the sun, moon, and stars. The heavens roll back as a scroll, the mountains and islands move out of their places, and men hide in the caves and rocks of the mountains because of the wrath of the Lamb, for "the great day of their wrath is come" (6:17). Keep in mind that this is not the lake of fire, but the day of wrath of the Great Tribulation.[12] Keep in mind also that the opening of this seven-sealed book does not take place until the first group of saints has been translated to meet the Lord in the air.

In the following chapter we shall see another group of people taken out of the Great Tribulation. This indicates that the rapture, like the day of the Lord, covers a *period* of time.[13] They both begin at the same time at the end of the church age. The rapture indicates a blessing; the day of the Lord indicates judgment. The rapture is for overcomers; the day of the Lord is for earth-dwellers. The rapture takes place at various intervals just before and during the Great Tribulation; the day of the Lord extends from the beginning of the Great Tribulation to the end of the millennial age.[14]

SUMMARY

In Revelation 6 Christ begins the conflict of the Great Tribulation period. The four horsemen start out with the Antichrist on the white horse, and he is followed by the red horse of war, the black horse of famine, and the pale horse of death. During this time many are martyred for the Word of God and for the testimony which they hold, and the chapter closes with the sixth seal of the great earthquake. Nothing is said about the seventh seal because of its multiple character (which we shall examine later) and because of a change of viewpoint. The focus in Chapter 7 is on two particular groups of people and what happens to them at the opening of the seals.

12/Cf. 1 Thess. 1:10.
13/Read Appendix 3.
14/Rev. 6:1—20:15.

CHRIST RESCUES IN THE CONFLICT

Revelation 7

Read Isaiah 54 as your devotional approach to this chapter, noting especially verses 1, 5-8, 14, and 17. Pray for wisdom and understanding. Then study Revelation 7 on your own. Be sure to use all the study techniques at your disposal, and update your charts as needed. To stimulate your personal study, ask yourself the following questions:

1. What is the mission of the four angels?
2. Why are they restrained from operating?
3. What does the fifth angel do? Why does he do it?
4. What does the seal of the living God imply?
5. Can you identify the two groups in this chapter? Who are they?
6. What is the location and significance of each group?
7. Can you connect the second group with any previously-mentioned group?
8. What are the rewards of the second group? Compare these with the rewards of the elders.

STUDY PROJECT NUMBER 6

Make a list of the twelve tribes of Israel in four parallel columns, using the following references for the heads of your columns:

1. *Birth*—Genesis 29, 30; 35:18.
2. *Egypt*—Genesis 46.
3. *Tribulation*—Revelation 7.
4. *Millennium*—Ezekiel 48.

Be sure to maintain the sequence of names in each list, then make significant observations about them.

NOTES ON REVELATION 7

The Christ who prepared for the conflict in Revelation 4 and 5 and opened the conflict in Chapter 6 now rescues two large groups of people in Chapter 7 by sealing 144,000 Jews and translating a great multitude of Gentiles during the terrors of the conflict.

THE SEALED JEWS (7:1-8)

The change of viewpoint in Revelation 7 is occasioned by the matchless mercy of Christ as he rescues two large groups of people in the conflict. Because of the awful judgments contained in the seventh judgment seal yet to be opened, it is imperative that the seal of the living God be placed on the 144,000 Israelites. This, in contrast to the seven seals of judgment, is the seal of ownership and preservation.[1]

The four angels of the four winds of universal judgment are commanded by a fifth angel to hold back further judgments until God's elect are sealed to pass through certain of these judgments. There is no hint that the number of these Israelites is symbolic, anymore than the number of the seven thousand people who had not bowed their knees to Baal[2]

[1]/Cf. Ezek. 9:4.
[2]/1 Kings 19:18; Rom. 11:26-36.

was symbolic. Nor is there any indication that these are the only Jews to be saved during the Great Tribulation. It does indicate, however, that these are the firstfruits of those Israelites who turn to God as a nation (14:4).

You will notice from your list of the twelve tribes suggested in Study Project Number 6 that Dan's name is omitted from Revelation 7. However, he is mentioned first in the millennial list of Ezekiel 48, presumably because he will have been rescued at a later time during the Great Tribulation. Ephraim is also omitted in Revelation 7, but by the grace of God he is mentioned along with Manasseh in Ezekiel 48. Because of Ephraim's terrible backsliding, God had said through Hosea, "Ephraim is joined to idols, let him alone" (Hos. 4: 17). This may account for his delay in returning to God at the end of the age.

Note that the Jews receive the seal of the living God *while they are on the earth*. Where are they in Chapter 14?

THE SAVED MULTITUDE (7:9-17)

The scene now changes from earth to heaven, and the setting is the same as in Chapters 4 and 5. This innumerable multitude includes people from every nation, tribe, people, and tongue. They stand before the central throne and the Lamb with palms in their hands and white robes on their bodies. Their ascription is "Salvation unto our God who sitteth on the throne, and unto the Lamb," and the angels, elders, and four living creatures respond with prostrate worship: "Amen; blessing, and glory, and wisdom, and thanksgiving, and honor, and power, and might be unto our God forever and ever. Amen" (7:12).

The double question asked by one of the elders, "Who are they, and whence came they?" is not intended to elicit an answer from John but to provide him with the correct information. John's answer, "My Lord, thou knowest," is tantamount to saying, "You tell me." The elder responds by saying that these saints have come out of the Great Tribulation. They are not to be identified with the 144,000 Israelites, for the descriptions of these two groups in Chapter 7 contrast sharply. Nor are they part of the firstfruits of the church represented by the elders, since one of the elders helps John identify these saints.

Then who are they? This great multitude represents the people who are living on the earth during the opening of the first six seals of judgment; they were left here during the first phase of the rapture. They were not ready when the Lord descended from heaven, so they were left to wash their robes and make them white in the blood of the Lamb. Being unprepared probably cost some of them their lives, for at least some of them may be identified with the souls under the altar in the fifth seal. Whether all or only some of them died, the implication is that they were all translated. So the rapture covers a period of time.

Notice also that they have no crowns, though they do carry palms of victory in their hands. They have no thrones, but they do serve God day and night in the temple. Not everything was lost because of missing the first translation. They are in heaven, they have white robes, they experience no more hunger or thirst, they have no sorrow or crying, and the Lamb is their Shepherd.

THE FIVE CROWNS

Five crowns are promised to the overcomer in the New Testament. The *first* is the crown of joy or rejoicing, given for faithfulness in soulwinning. "Wherefore, my brethren beloved and longed for, my joy and crown, so stand fast in the Lord, my beloved" (Phil. 4:1).

The *second* is the crown of righteousness, given for faithfulness in daily living. "Henceforth there is laid up for me the crown of righteousness, which the Lord, the righteous judge, shall give to me at that day; and not to me only, but also to all them that have loved his appearing" (2 Tim. 4:8).

The *third* is the crown of life, given for faithfulness under trial. "Blessed is the man that endureth temptation, for when he hath been approved he shall receive the crown of life, which the Lord promised to them that love him" (James 1:12). "Fear not the things which thou art about to suffer; behold, the devil is about to cast some of you into prison, that ye may be tried; and you shall have tribulation ten days. Be thou faithful unto death, and I will give thee the crown of life" (Rev. 2:10).

The *fourth* is the crown of glory, given for faithfulness under suffering. "And when the chief Shepherd shall be manifested, ye shall receive the crown of glory that fadeth not away" (1 Pet. 5:4). "But we behold him who hath been made a little lower than the angels, even Jesus, because of the suffering of death crowned with glory and honor, that by the grace of God he should taste death for every man" (Heb. 2:9).

The *fifth* is the crown incorruptible, given for faithfulness in temptation. "Know ye not that they that run in a race run all, but one receiveth the prize? Even so run, that ye may attain. And every man that striveth in the games exerciseth self-control in all things. Now they do it to receive a corruptible crown, but we an incorruptible" (1 Cor. 9:24, 25).

SUMMARY

We have seen that the change in viewpoint in Chapter 7 shows how Christ rescues two large groups in the conflict. In his great mercy he delays the opening of the seventh seal of judgment until 144,000 of his elect are set apart by the seal of the living God and until a great multitude of Gentiles are taken out of the Great Tribulation. Since all this occurs near the *end* of the first half of the Great Tribulation, and since the elders and living creatures are seen in heaven *before* the Great Tribulation, we conclude that the rapture covers a period of time.

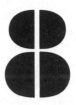

CHRIST JUDGES IN THE CONFLICT

Revelation 8, 9

INSTRUCTIONS FOR STUDYING REVELATION 8 AND 9

Read Revelation 8:1 as your devotional approach to these awful judgments, asking the Lord not merely to make you worthy to escape but also to burden you about the careless souls who are unconcerned about escaping. Follow the recommended steps of study; do not omit any. There are no shortcuts to Bible knowledge! This kind of independent study pays large dividends in eternal values. Let the following questions help you in your independent study.

1. Why the unique silence in heaven described in 8:1? Contrast 4:8; 5:13; 7:11, 12.
2. What is the source of the judgments in Chapters 8 and 9?
3. How are the trumpet judgments related to the seal judgments?
4. What is the difference, if any, between the altar of incense in 8:3 and the altar in 6:9?
5. What is the significance of the altar, the incense, the smoke, and the fire cast to the earth?
6. Where is the division in the sequence of the seven trumpets? Why is it here?

7. What is the reason for these awful trumpet judgments?
8. What is the bottomless pit? Where is it? See Luke 8:27-31.
9. Compare the "seal of God" in 9:4 and 7:2. What is its significance?
10. What are the source, duration, and mercy of the second woe of 9:13-21? Compare Jeremiah 51:60-64.
11. What is the attitude of the human heart in 9:20, 21? How is this significant?

STUDY PROJECT NUMBER 7

It is common knowledge that Satan fell from his original position of glory through pride and self-will. List the five assertions of Satanic self-will described in Isaiah 14. Now begin your list of Satan's four steps of degradation, beginning with his expulsion from heaven and ending with his final abode described in Revelation.

NOTES ON REVELATION 8, 9

The Christ who prepared for the conflict in Revelation 4 and 5, who opened the conflict in Chapter 6, and who rescued two large groups of people in Chapter 7 now judges in the conflict in Chapters 8 and 9, sounding six of the seven trumpets of judgment.

THE SEVENTH SEAL (8:1-5)

Now that God has lovingly sealed 144,000 Jews and mercifully translated a great multitude of Gentiles out of the Great Tribulation, the slain Lamb resumes the opening of the judgment seals. There is apparently only one seal left, the seventh, but when this seal is broken there follows a half-hour of absolute silence in all heaven. There are no doxologies, no ascriptions of praise, and no expressions of worship. It is like the hush before the sudden burst of a destructive storm. God the Father, the slain Lamb, the twenty-four elders, the four living creatures, the great multitude of tribulation saints, and the myriads of angels all wait in awesome silence. The only movement seems to be the seven flashing torches of the Holy Spirit and the sparkling glory of the enthroned Father. But soon the silent characters will move into action, for the Christ who *rescued* in the conflict will now *judge* in the conflict. The judgments of the seventh seal are more terrible than the preceding ones, for they are multiple. The awful stillness in heaven reaches its climax as the decimating judgments of the seventh seal are revealed.

Then the action of the throne resumes. Seven angels come before God to receive seven trumpets. Another angel with a golden censer is given much incense to add to the prayers of all the saints on the golden altar, and he casts fire from the altar down to earth. This results in a general upheaval of the elements, manifested by thunders, voices, lightnings, and an earthquake. Then the incense is placed on the altar, the place of prayer and communion, in order to make the prayers of the saints acceptable to God. The prayer "Thy kingdom come; thy will be done, as in heaven, so on earth" is now being answered, for the world is being prepared for the reign of Christ. The prayers of the souls under the altar (6:9, 10) are being answered too, for the seventh seal contains the soon-to-be-sounded seven judgment trumpets. These judgments divide into four and three, with the first four physical in character and the last three (the woe trumpets) produced by spiritual forces.

ONE-THIRD OF THE EARTH BURNED (8:6, 7)

When the *first trumpet* is sounded by the first angel, hail and fire mingled with blood are cast on the earth. Flames destroy one-third of the earth's consumables, including one-third of the trees and other vegetation. Since no symbolism is implied, the description of this judgment should be taken literally.

ONE-THIRD OF THE SEA BLOOD (8:8, 9)

At the blasting of the *second trumpet* something like a great burning mountain is cast into the sea. One-third of the sea turns into blood, one-third of its marine life dies, and one-third of its ships are destroyed. What is the purpose of all this destruction? Isaiah says, "When thy judgments are in the earth, the inhabitants of the world learn righteousness" (26: 9).

ONE-THIRD OF THE RIVERS AND FOUNTAINS BITTER (8:10, 11)

After the blowing of the *third trumpet* a great burning star is cast into the sea. The name of this star, Wormwood, reveals its character and purpose, for wormwood is the bitterest shrub known. As in the episode at Marah (Exod. 15:23), one-third of the rivers and fountains become bitter, and many people die of thirst. Seiss tells of a great volcanic explosion in one of the Aleutian Islands on March 21, 1823, in which river water assumed the color of beer and became so extremely bitter as to be unfit for use.[1] God does not lack for means to accomplish his desired ends! The problem of pollution today shows that these things can really happen. There is not a single fish still alive in Lake Erie, and a number of scientists say that large areas of the earth will be habitable for only another ten years unless abuse of our natural environment is radically curbed. Self-extinction through the relentless ravages of pollution may easily become the inevitable fate of man. Add to this the supernatural power of God, and we have every reason to believe that every prophecy in Revelation will be literally fulfilled!

ONE-THIRD OF THE HEAVENLY BODIES DARKENED (8:12, 13)

The fourth judgment is the counterpart of the fourth day of creation, when God said "Let there be light-bearers," for

---

1/Seiss, *op. cit.*, p. 197. Cf. Jer. 9:13-15.

the blowing of the *fourth trumpet* brings midnight darkness. One-third of the sun, moon, and stars are smitten, and there is darkness during one-third of the day and night. These four trumpet judgments are really only preliminaries to the three woe trumpets to follow, for these three woes are announced by an eagle flying in mid-heaven with the warning, "Woe, woe, woe for them that dwell on the earth by reason of the other voices of the trumpet of the three angels who are yet to sound" (8:13).

THE STAR-LOCUST WOE (9:1-12)

The sounding of the *fifth trumpet* is called the *first woe*— the star-locust woe. Here God uses the fallen star as his tool of punishment. Since this star is given authority to unlock the pit or shaft of the abyss, it is not hard to identify him as Satan.[2] The angelic beings locked in the abyss are angels who sinned and "kept not their first estate."[3] There are various degrees and orders among fallen creatures,[4] and Satan is called "the prince of the powers of the air."[5]

When Satan opens the pit of the abyss, great billows of smoke burst forth to darken the sun and the air. Out of this smoke come supernatural "locusts" with power to sting like scorpions. These infernal beings have the combined characteristics of locusts, scorpions, horses, lions, and human beings. Their king, Apollyon, is the angel of the abyss, and his name means "destroyer." His destructive power, however, is limited by the sovereign God. Just as Satan was not allowed to kill Job, so this destroyer is not allowed to kill men. He is not allowed to even touch the sealed Jews (9:4). However, most earth-dwellers are so tormented by the destroyer that they wish to die, but death eludes them for five long months of torture.

2/Luke 10:18; Rev. 12:9; see page 113.
3/2 Pet. 2:4; Jude 6 KJV.
4/Eph. 6:12; Col. 2:15; Matt. 25:41.
5/Eph. 2:2.

THE 200-MILLION-HORSEMAN WOE (9:13-21)

The sounding of the *sixth trumpet* is called the *second woe*—the 200-million-horseman woe. Here the Christ in conflict releases other Satanic beings that have been bound in the region of the great Euphrates River. This region once produced some of the greatest ancient world powers, such as Assyria, Babylonia, and Persia. These spread their devastating dominion over the entire world and overpowered God's chosen people. Revelation 9 implies that certain fallen angels have been bound in the lowest part of the abyss[6] until this exact day, so that upon their release they may burn and suffocate one-third of the people still left on the earth. Those they do not kill they hurt with the stings in their tails.

Though the purpose of this second woe is partly retributive and partly reformatory, "the rest of mankind, who were not killed with these plagues, repented not" (9:20). They continued worshipping demons and idols, and they continued their murders, sorceries, fornications, and thefts. Men who do not repent under mercy are not likely to repent under judgment!

SUMMARY

We have seen how Christ in the conflict resumed his role as Judge in Chapters 8 and 9 by opening the seventh seal, for instead of terminating the judgments, this seventh seal unleashed seven more terrible judgments. The first four were physical in character and burned one-third of the earth, bloodied one-third of the sea, embittered one-third of the fresh water sources, and darkened one-third of the heavenly bodies.

The last three trumpet judgments were produced by spiritual forces. The two woe trumpets sounded in Chapter 9 produced the star-locust woe and the 200-million-horseman woe. The third woe, or seventh trumpet, is mercifully postponed until a later time.

6/2 Pet. 2:4.

CHRIST PRECIPITATES THE CONFLICT

Revelation 10, 11

INSTRUCTIONS FOR STUDYING REVELATION 10 AND 11

Read Psalm 34 as your devotional approach, and pray for deliverance. Study Revelation 10 and 11 intensively on your own, then try to answer the following questions.

1. What happened to the seventh trumpet of Chapters 8 and 9?
2. What has the author accomplished in Chapters 8 through 11?
3. Who is the strong angel? What is the problem of his identification?
4. What does the strong angel do?
5. Can you identify the little book?
6. What is the full significance of 10:7? Keep looking at this verse until you can see its relationship to both the immediate and remote contexts. Relate 10:7 to Chapter 11, then to the progress of the whole book.
7. Compare 10:9, 10 with Ezekiel 3:1-4.
8. What is the significance of the measuring rod in 11:1?
9. What is the ministry of the two witnesses? Can you identify them?

10. What is the significance of the 42 months in 11:2? Compare this verse with Daniel 9:27.
11. Is the temple in 11:1 the same as the temple in 11:19?
12. What happens to the two witnesses when they have finished their testimony? Compare 11:12 with 4:1.
13. Evaluate the reaction of the enemies of the two witnesses in 11:13.
14. Does Chapter 11 complete the narrative begun in Chapter 8? Explain.
15. What events are covered by the seventh trumpet? What period of time is covered?

NOTES ON REVELATION 10, 11

THE CONSUMMATION ANNOUNCED (10:1-11)

The Christ who prepared for the conflict in Chapters 4 and 5, who opened the conflict in Chapter 6, who rescued his chosen groups in Chapter 7, and who effected six of the seven judgments in Chapters 8 and 9 now precipitates the conflict in Chapters 10 and 11 by announcing the final consummation.

The Strong Angel (10:1-7)

Chapter 10 represents a change of viewpoint from heaven to earth,[1] but John is still viewing the same second "showing" which began in Chapter 4. Revelation 10:4 indicates that John recorded the visions when he saw them rather than at a later date, for "when the seven thunders uttered their voices, I was about to write," said John.

The scene in 10:1-7 opens in time for John to see "another strong angel" come down out of heaven (10:1). Who is he? There are two possible answers. One interpretation makes him simply a herald angel of the great things that belong to the seventh trumpet. In this view he is very much like the "strong angel" in 5:2, "another angel" in 8:3, and

---

1/Rev. 10:1, 2, 8; 11:1.

"another angel" in 18:1. Those who hold this view say that "one like unto a son of man" (1:13; 14:14) would not likely appear here as an angel. A third reason is based on 10:6: "And sware by him that liveth forever and ever, who created the heaven and the things that are therein, and the earth and the things that are therein, and the sea and the things that are therein." But in Hebrews 6:13 God swore by himself because he could find no greater personage.

A more plausible interpretation identifies the strong angel of 10:1 as Christ himself. Several arguments support this view. First, the attire of this angel indicates Deity. He is arrayed with a cloud, the rainbow is on his head, his face is as the sun, and his feet are as pillars of fire. Christ is described this way in Revelation 1. Second, the definite article used with "rainbow" points out individual identity and particularizes the Greek noun. This seems to indicate that this rainbow is the same one surrounding the throne in 4:3. Third, the strong angel has a small opened book in his hand, and this book should probably be identified with the seven-sealed book of Chapter 5 (the title deed to the earth). It would be strange indeed if so important a book were never mentioned again. The fact that it is now open instead of sealed harmonizes with the fact that the seventh seal has been broken (8:1). The objection to this view is that a different word is used for the book here (*biblarídion,* 10:2, 9, 10) than is used in Chapter 5 (*biblíon,* vv. 1, 2, 3, 4, 5, 8, 9). But *biblíon* also occurs in verse 8 of Chapter 10, and the forms used in both chapters are simply diminutive forms of *bíblos* and mean practically the same thing. Fourth, the strong angel claims possession of the sea and of the earth, suggesting Christ rather than a mere angel. Fifth, the strong angel cries with a great voice of a roaring lion, and this mighty cry is echoed by seven thunders. This may be identified with the Lion of the tribe of Judah[2] in Chapter 5. The representation of Christ under the figure "another strong angel" is similar to his frequent title in the Old Testament, "the angel of Jehovah."[3]

2/Rev. 5:5; cf. Jer. 25:30.
3/Gen. 16:7 and throughout the O.T.

This strong angel makes one of the most far-reaching announcements in the Revelation. The announcement is prefaced by a solemn oath to "him that liveth forever and ever," and the reason for the announcement is that "there shall be delay no longer" (10:6). So we are entering into a new phase of divine judgment.[4] Previously the scoffers had taunted, "Where is the promise of his coming? For from the day that the fathers fell asleep, all things continue as they were from the beginning of the creation" (2 Pet. 3:4).

After these introductory words the angel announces, "In the days of the voice of the seventh angel, when he is about to sound, then is finished the mystery of God, according to the good tidings which he declared to his servants the prophets" (10:7). Every word of this blazing headline is pregnant with meaning.

"Days" indicates a period of time rather than a single event. "About to sound" indicates the imminence of this last part of the Great Tribulation. "Finished" indicates the completion of all prophecy—the last half of the Great Tribulation, the entire millennial reign of Christ, and the beginning of the eternal ages. The events included in this great announcement are listed in 11:15-19. (This is a good illustration of the law of recurrence. Where can we find a further description of the events of 11:19?) Note that "the mystery of God" (10:7) is in contrast to "the revelation of Jesus Christ" (1:1). Seiss says,

> The mystery of God is nothing more or less than the final sum of all God's revelations and doings for the reinstatement of man into his lost inheritance. The fulfilment of this mystery is the final accomplishment of the last items of the divine administrations which make up that sum—the ultimate realization of all of the foreannouncements made to and by any and every one of God's prophets in all of the ages—the gospel of the kingdom of heaven at length merged into full and everlasting fruition of that kingdom—the consummation of all things.[5]

4/Cf. Ezek. 12:25, 28.
5/Seiss, *op. cit.*, pp. 229, 230.

So in the Book of Revelation we find the unfolding of the mystery of God and the finishing of all prophecy.

The Little Book (10:8-11)

One reason for identifying the strong angel of 10:1 as Christ is that the "little book open" of 10:2 is probably the seven-sealed book or title deed to the earth that the worthy Lamb began to open in Chapter 6. If this identification is correct, Revelation 10 records the ultimate disposal of this most important document.

John is commanded to take the book and eat it up.[6] Though it is sweet as honey in his mouth,[7] in his belly it becomes bitter. In our own experience it is sweet to hear the Word of God but often bitter to obey some of its more difficult requirements. Who would understand this better than John, who was at that very moment exiled on the Isle of Patmos for the Word of God and the testimony of Jesus! Yet John's ministry was not yet finished, for God's commission continues, "Thou must prophesy again over many peoples and nations and tongues and kings" (10:11).

THE EARTHLY TEMPLE (11:1, 2)

Beginning with Revelation 11, John's role is changed from that of a seer and scribe to that of an actor. In Chapter 10 John took the open book, ate it, and received the commission to prophesy. Here in Chapter 11 John is told by "One" (Christ) to "Rise and measure the temple of God and the altar and them that worship therein" (11:1). Seiss says,

> He [John] acts the part in the apocalyptic scenes which pertain to the whole body to which he belongs. What is given him in the vision is to be understood as given them, and what he does and experiences is to be understood as done and experienced by them, when the vision becomes reality.[8]

6/Cf. Ezek. 3.
7/Psalm 19:10.
8/Seiss, *op. cit.,* p. 234.

In other words, John represents the church which is in heaven
at the time the vision is fulfilled. These resurrected, translated, and glorified saints are given the title deed to the earth.
The eating of this book enables them to witness for God to
"many peoples and nations and tongues and kings" (10:11).
The nature of this witnessing is administrative. "Know ye not
that the saints shall judge the world?" (1 Cor. 6:2).

Here their special work is to measure the temple[9] and
altar of God and those who worship there. Measuring is both a
judicial act and a sign of ownership. Since judgment must
begin at the house of God, the place of worship and the worshippers themselves are measured first. So God is now evaluat-
ing his chosen people, the Jews. This is the primary purpose
of the Great Tribulation. By this time the ancient temple will
have been rebuilt in Jerusalem,[10] and among the worshippers
will be many true servants of God. In Revelation 7, the
144,000 Jews were singled out as objects of his gracious protection, and in Chapter 14 they will be translated safely into
the presence of God.

Before this translation, however, there will be much chastisement. "Zion shall be redeemed with justice, and her con-
verts with righteousness" (Isa. 1:27). Note that the measuring is done with a reed "like unto a rod," and not with a
"golden reed," as is used to measure the New Jerusalem (21:
15). This measuring rod implies not only ownership but
chastisement. What will be the source of the chastening?

9/The word for temple here is *naós,* indicating the sanctuary or holy
of holies—not *hierón,* which includes the courts. The courts of the
priests, of men, and of women were separated from the outer court by
a wall with an inscription forbidding entry by any Gentile on pain of
death.
10/Solomon's temple was destroyed by Nebuchadnezzar in 586 B.C.
Zerubbabel's temple, which was built in 516 B.C. and was pillaged by
Antiochus Epiphanes in 168 B.C. (Ezra 6:15), was number two. Herod's
enlarged temple was begun about 20 B.C. It was completely demolished
by the soldiers of Titus in A.D. 70. The Mohammedan Mosque called
the Dome of the Rock now occupies the place where the sanctuary once
stood. This temple area is about 25 acres, and the Prophet Mohammed
is supposed to have ascended to heaven on his white steed from this
spot. That is why the temple site is so sacred to the Arab that even
today he will not allow a Jew to put his foot on it.

"And the court which is without the temple leave without, and measure it not, for it hath been given unto the nations; and the holy city shall they tread under foot forty and two months" (11:2). So the pressure will come from the Gentiles until "the fulness of the Gentiles be come in" (Rom. 11:25), and the last half of the Great Tribulation will be the worst chastisement of all. "I will bring the third part into the fire, and will refine them as silver is refined, and will try them as gold is tried" (Zech. 13:9). The breaking of the seven-year covenant with the Jews by the Antichrist in the middle of the Great Tribulation[11] will be followed by the trampling underfoot of the Holy City for 42 months.

THE TWO WITNESSES (11:3-14)

But God in his grace has made advance plans, for during these 42 months (1260 days) the two witnesses prophesy while clothed in sackcloth. They are called "the two olive trees and the two candlesticks (lampstands), standing before the Lord of the earth" (11:4). Both the Law and the Gospels call for two witnesses to establish important truth,[12] and in both Old and New Testaments God sends out his witnesses in pairs: Moses and Aaron, Caleb and Joshua, Zerubbabel and Joshua, the twelve apostles, and the seventy.

Who are these two witnesses? Practically all commentators refer to the vision in Zechariah 4 and the words of the angel who gave it: "This is the word of the Lord unto Zerubbabel, saying, Not by might, nor by power, but by my Spirit, saith the Lord of Hosts." So the restoration of Jerusalem and its temple by Zerubbabel in 516 B.C. was to be accomplished by supernatural power.

Here in Revelation, however, the picture is different from that of Zechariah's day. The golden candlestick with its seven lamps, seven pipes, and seven bowls has disappeared. The church age has also ended, and the gospel ministers are missing. Only the two witnesses bear testimony to God on the

---

11/Dan. 9:24-27.
12/Deut. 17:6; Matt. 18:16.

eve of this plunge into the deepest waters of the Great Tribulation. But these two witnesses have supernatural power to burn men who desire to hurt them, to shut the heaven so that it does not rain, to turn water into blood, and to smite the earth with every plague at their own discretion. It is obvious that these powers do not characterize the church age, either in the ministry of Christ or the ministry of the apostles. But these powers do remind us of the ministries of Moses and Elijah (some say Enoch and Elijah). Although no one can be sure of the identification of the two witnesses, here are some reasons for suggesting they are Moses and Elijah. First, God called each of these men to lead his people at a time when his work on earth depended largely on a single man. Second, the ministry of the two witnesses is very similar to that of Moses and Elijah.[13] Third, because of the prophecy of Malachi 4:5, Jews and Christians alike have expected Elijah to return before Christ's final return to earth. Fourth, both Moses and Elijah appeared on the Mount of Transfiguration, suggesting that they will have a special part in the coming kingdom.[14]

The two witnesses of Revelation 11:3-13 are immortal until their work is done, but after they finish their testimony the Beast "that cometh up out of the abyss shall make war with them, and overcome them, and kill them. And their dead bodies lie in the street of the great city, which spiritually is called Sodom and Egypt, where also their Lord was crucified"

---

[13]/Exod. 7:19; 1 Kings 17.

[14]/A few Bible teachers insist that one of the witnesses is Enoch rather than Moses, reasoning that since Enoch did not die, he must come back and be killed. The Scripture used to support this view is "And inasmuch as it is appointed unto men *once* to die, and after this cometh the judgment; so Christ also, having been *once* offered to bear the sins of many, shall appear a second time, apart from sin, to them that wait for him, unto salvation" (Heb. 9:27, 28). The contrast in these verses, however, is between the repeated offerings of the Old Covenant and the once-for-all offering of Christ. The main message of this passage is that Christ will appear a second time—not that all must die. In fact, those saints, who are alive at the time of Christ's coming will never die (1 Thess. 4:16, 17). Although no one can be dogmatic as to the identity of the two witnesses in Revelation, the writer favors Moses as one of the witnesses rather than Enoch. Most Bible scholars seem to agree that the other witness is Elijah.

(11:7, 8). The mention of the Beast shows that this narrative is somewhat anticipative, for the work of the Beast is not fully described until Chapter 13. (This is another illustration of the law of recurrence.) It is important to note that throughout the rest of the Great Tribulation these two witnesses are on duty. Near the end of 1260 days they are overcome and killed by the Beast, and their dead bodies lie in the street 3½ days (11:8, 9). Burial is denied them, and as Newell says, "A regular Christmastime-of-hell ensues."[15] The earth-dwellers celebrate and send gifts to each other, but their time of merriment ends abruptly after 3½ days, for the breath of God resurrects the two witnesses and the call of God translates them to heaven.[16]

Note that there have been three translations to heaven up to this point: John (representing the overcomers, 4:1), the great multitude (7:14), and the two witnesses (11:12). It is interesting to observe that these three translations represent three current tribulational viewpoints—pretribulationism, midtribulationism, and posttribulationism. But the biblical viewpoint combines all three!

The result of Christ's ascension was consolation by angels,[17] but the result of the witnesses' translation is judgment. A great earthquake levels a tenth of the city, and seven thousand people die (11:13). The terrified survivors then glorify the God of heaven. They are not necessarily converted, however, for most of them continue their iniquities and their service to the Beast.[18]

THE SEVENTH TRUMPET (11:15-18)

Because the death and resurrection of the two witnesses occurs at the end of the Great Tribulation, Christ uses the following verses (11:15-18) to paint a composite picture of events through the millennial reign of Christ. This means

---

[15]/Newell, *op. cit.,* p. 155.
[16]/Rev. 11:11, 12; cf. 4:1.
[17]/Acts 1:10, 11.
[18]/Cf. Rev. 9:20.

that *the third woe announces the consummation.* In other words, the period covered by the seventh trumpet covers more than a thousand years (cf. 10:7). This thousand-year period includes the following events:

1. The millennial and eternal reign of Christ.
2. The reign of the saints (enthroned elders).
3. The worship of Christ by the saints.[19]
4. The campaign of Armageddon (past).
5. The judgment of the dead—saints and sinners.

The worship of Christ by the elders reminds us that the scene described in Chapters 4 and 5 is still the main backdrop for the "showing," and that these representatives of the firstborn of the resurrection—these seniors of the celestial congregation of the redeemed—sympathize fully with the saints still on the earth or in the grave. When Christ ultimately takes the reins of world government the elders fall on their faces and worship God with the words, "We give thee thanks, O Lord God, the Almighty, who art and who wast, because thou hast taken thy great power and didst reign" (11:17).

THE HEAVENLY TEMPLE (11:19)

In contrast to the earthly temple of 11:1, 2, in verse 19 the heavenly temple is opened. The mention of the ark of the covenant reminds us that this object was a very sacred piece of furniture in the ancient temple of the Jews, and that they believed it would be brought back in the day of Israel's blessing. Here in Revelation 11 the ark represents God's holy presence, as shown by the "lightnings, and voices, and thunders, and an earthquake, and great hail" (verse 19).

The brief description of the heavenly temple would seem strange were it not for the fuller explanation of its significance in Chapters 15 and 16. The full details of the consummation are announced in later chapters even though certain events take place in the time context of Chapter 11.

19/Notice that in the worship of Christ by the elders they do not add "the One coming," as in 1:4, 8, for Christ has already come! Compare 4:8 and 16:5.

SUMMARY

We have seen how Christ precipitated the conflict by announcing the consummation, by instructing John to measure the earthly temple, by prophesying through his two witnesses, by sounding the seventh trumpet, and by opening the heavenly temple. There is still much repossessing of the earth to be accomplished, and Christ's victory over Satan at Calvary will be consummated in later chapters of Revelation.

10

CHRIST DELIVERS IN THE CONFLICT

Revelation 12

INSTRUCTIONS FOR STUDYING REVELATION 12

Read Psalm 40:1-5 as your devotional approach, and thank God for bringing you out of the horrible pit and placing you on the rock. Then study Revelation 12 and record your findings. Remember to update your charts and projects. Let the following questions help you think through this wonderful chapter.

1. How are the laws of repetition and recurrence illustrated in Revelation 12?
2. What previous chapter is parallel in time to Chapter 12?
3. What is the key word of Chapter 12, and how does it help you understand the symbols?
4. Are the symbols too sweeping for the strictly futuristic viewpoint?
5. Are all the personages of Chapter 12 symbolic? Explain.
6. Describe all aspects of the woman.
7. Who is the woman's enemy? Who is her son?
8. What is her problem? What is her son's problem? What is God's solution?

9. What is the nature of the war? Where is it fought? What is the result?
10. What is the significance of the period of days?
11. When will verse 12 be fulfilled?
12. When will the woman be persecuted?
13. Is the river of water literal or figurative? Why? Compare Numbers 16:32.
14. Who is the seed of the woman?
15. What is the key verse of Chapter 12?
16. Did you have trouble naming the paragraphs? If so, why not make your own divisions?

Read the rest of this chapter only after you have completed your independent study.

NOTES ON REVELATION 12

THE SUN-CLOTHED WOMAN (12:1, 2)

The Christ who prepared for the conflict in Revelation 4 and 5, who opened the conflict in Chapter 6, who rescued his chosen groups in Chapter 7, who effected six of the seven trumpet judgments in Chapters 8 and 9, and who precipitated the conflict in Chapter 10 and 11 now delivers the sun-clothed woman and her man-child in Chapter 12.

Revelation 12 is one of the most comprehensive chapters in the whole Bible, for its implications sweep from Genesis to the end of Revelation. The first indication of this mighty span is the verb "was seen" (*ōphthē*) in verse 1. John does not say that he "saw," as in his previous visions, but that "a great sign *was seen* in heaven" (12:1). So John was not the only personage who saw the sign. The identity of the various other personages who saw this sign will become clearer to us as we delve into the chapter.

Though the words "in heaven" imply "from the heavenly viewpoint," the scene of the vision seems to be as much on earth as in heaven. Revelation 12 is the first example of John's overlapping chronology, for the time element of this chapter is the same as that of Chapter 4. This will become clearer as we analyze the pertinent events and persons.

Her Significance

Since the sun-clothed woman is called a "sign" (*sēmeíon*) in verse 1, we should interpret her identity symbolically. The word "sign" is one of the key words of Revelation, and it appears a total of 77 times throughout the New Testament. Here the word indicates that the prophetic message of this particular section is being conveyed pictorially. (However, since the word "sign" is not used in connection with Michael [verse 7], he should undoubtedly be identified literally.)

Her Clothing

We should also notice that the sun-clothed woman's outer garment is the sun, her footstool is the moon, and her crown is twelve stars. With the sun thrown around her, this glorious woman holds a victorious position in the heavenlies and acts as a lightbearer to the world. With the moon under her feet she is victorious over the powers of darkness, even as the moon is the queen of the night. Her victorious position is the same as that of the church in Ephesians. The first three chapters of Ephesians describe the church seated in the heavenlies and the last three chapters present her walking on the earth. This position enables her to conquer every foe and to fulfill her role as the light of the world. If the twelve stars in the woman's crown represent God's anointed ones or ministers,[1] this is yet another indication that the woman represents a group rather than an individual.

Her Condition

The sun-clothed woman is pregnant and will soon experience the joy of delivering a son, a male! The imminent hope of the child's delivery is the third indication that the woman represents more than a single individual. Both Israel and the New Testament church are represented in Scripture

---

1/Dan. 12:3; 1 Pet. 2:9; Rev. 1:6-20.

under the figure of motherhood. In fact, "the whole creation groaneth and travaileth in pain together until now . . . waiting for . . . the redemption of our body" (Rom. 8:22, 23). These observations lead us to conclude that the woman represents the people of God in both Testaments, beginning with righteous Abel and ending with the last saint to be saved before the reign of Christ. So the woman "was seen" by more people than John. On the other hand, since John also saw her in his vision of the *future,* it is important to note that in this particular context the woman represents the visible and invisible church at the first "catching up" and for most of the Great Tribulation period thereafter. This will become clearer as we examine her son and her seed.

THE GREAT RED DRAGON (12:3, 4)

His Significance

The great red Dragon is also called a "sign," so we should identify him figuratively, too. Actually no such literal animal exists, and Christ himself explains the figure fully in verse 9. The Dragon is identified as the Old Serpent, the Devil, Satan, the deceiver of the whole world, and the accuser of the brethren. But this identification would not have been difficult even if the meaning had not been given, for the dragon was often employed in ancient literature as a symbol of evil. Here he represents the horror and tragedy that sin brings through the works of the Devil.

His Description

When compared with his former state described in Ezekiel 28:12-19, Satan's very appearance now shows the awful consequences of his pride and self-will. "Red" (verse 3) suggests his murderous character from the beginning to the end.[2] This aspect is highlighted in the second horseman of Revelation 6. His seven heads and seven diadems (12:3) indicate the arrogant assumption of glory that belongs to God

---

[2]/Cf. John 8:44; Rev. 20:7, 8.

alone. His ten horns indicate power, and in Chapter 13 he projects this power through the Beast to the ten-king world government.

His Deeds

The deeds of the Dragon include drawing a third of the stars of heaven and casting them to the earth. Since this whole picture is a sign, the stars are also figurative. Jude speaks of "angels that kept not their own principality, but left their proper habitation" (Jude 6), and Peter says, "God spared not angels when they sinned" (2 Pet. 2:4). This pre-adamic rebellion in heaven resulted in *the first step in the degradation of Satan and his hosts*.[3] When he was cast out of heaven because of his sin, Satan drew one-third of the angels with him in his presumptuous cause. This is history, and it shows the all-inclusive scope of the scenes in Revelation 12. The first step in Satan's degradation takes him from God's presence to the "heavenly places" (Eph. 6:12), but now he is forced to take his *second step*, this time to the earth.[4] Another historical aspect of the deeds of Satan is his many attempts throughout history to kill God's people. Recall Cain and Abel, Pharaoh and the children of Israel, Saul and David, Ahasuerus and the Jews, Herod and Christ, and the persecuted Christians throughout the church age. These cases from history are included in this vision of Revelation 12. But what about the *future* aspect of this great Dragon's deeds? Here he stands before the pregnant woman, waiting to devour her child. It is important to see that this act is a part of the future conflict.

His Names

The first alternate name for the Dragon is the "Old Serpent" (12:9). This familiar figure originated in Genesis 3. Satan used a serpent to deceive Eve and curse the entire human race. He is also called the "Devil," a name which is always used in the singular in the original languages of the Bi-

---

3/Rev. 9:1; Eph. 6:12.
4/Rev. 12:9.

ble. Thank God there is only one Devil! "Devil" and "Satan" ("Adversary") are the names used most often in the Bible to indicate this chief of the fallen spirits. "The deceiver of the whole world" and "the accuser of our brethren" (12:9, 10) are names that tell their own story. Satan would like to deceive, if possible, the very elect,[5] and he carries on this work from Genesis 3 to Revelation 20. His false accusations also span the same period.

THE SON, A MALE (12:5, 6)

His Names

Since the soon-to-be-delivered child is part of the symbol of the woman, the word "sign" applies to him also. Who is this child? His names provide the first clue. Verse 5 says that he is a son (*huiós,* masculine singular), a male (*ársen,* neuter singular). This Greek combination of genders does not occur in English. The neuter singular is used collectively to refer to persons related to the individual named by the masculine.[6] Who else could this be but *Christ and his Church?*

Notice the comprehensiveness of the figure. It is true that Christ came from the Jews, but certainly the woman and her child represent more than Israel and Christ. Both history and prophecy are involved. Just as the figure of the woman is comprehensive and culminative, so is the figure of her son, a male. Historically he represents Christ, but prophetically he

---

[5]/Matt. 24:24.

[6]/Other instances are found in John 6:37 and 2 Thess. 2:6, 7. "All that which (neuter singular) the Father giveth me" refers to all who have been predestined to eternal life, and "him that cometh to me (masculine singular) refers to the individual who actually does the coming. In 2 Thess. "that which restraineth" (neuter singular) refers to that group of people whose very presence in the world is hindering the revelation of the Man of Sin, and "the one that restrains" (masculine singular) refers to the restraining power of an individual personality in the world "until he gets out of the way" (deponent middle form, *génetai,* used in the active sense). This is the strongest kind of evidence that *the restrainer is the church as indwelt by the Holy Spirit.* See page 83.

represents the firstfruits company of saints depicted in Revelation 4—John, the twenty-four elders, and the four living creatures. Just as John heard the invitation "Come up hither," so the son, a male, "was caught up unto God, and unto his throne" (12:5). This son represents the overcomers mentioned throughout Revelation 2 and 3. They are part of the true church, that invisible spiritual body united to God by faith in Christ.

His Work

The male-child is destined to "rule all the nations with a rod of iron" (verse 5). How perfectly this harmonizes with Christ as the Head, and the Church as his body! Listen to the promise which Christ gave to the overcomer in his message to Thyatira: "He that overcometh, and he that keepeth my works unto the end, to him will I give authority over the nations; and he shall rule them with a rod of iron" (2:26, 27). Here in Chapter 12 the overcomers are represented under the unique figure of a neuter male, picturing strength and manliness. Thus the man-child destined to rule all nations includes both Christ and his saints, both the Head and the body.

THE ARCHANGEL MICHAEL (12:7-12)

His Identity

Since the word "sign" is not used of Michael, we should identify him as a literal archangel. The angel who communicated with Daniel labeled Michael "one of the chief princes" (Dan. 10:13) and Jude described him as the archangel who refused to make a slanderous accusation against Satan (Jude 9). According to Jewish tradition Michael is the chief of the seven archangels.

His Work

As the very chief of all angels, Michael would be the proper personage to lead the great army of heaven against the Dragon and his forces. Michael's objective is to protect both the sun-clothed woman (representing the church as a visible body) and her newborn son (representing the invisible church). As the forces of Michael and Satan meet, a war ensues in heaven (verse 7). The nature of the conflict, however, is spiritual rather than physical. There is no bloodshed or loss of life, for the battle is in the realm of the moral, intellectual, and spiritual. Seiss says,

> The canonading is thought, argument, subtle accusation, and defense. It is a war of mind with mind, of malignant and hellish intellect inflamed with desperate hate and anger against the intellect, reason, and right of heaven, a war which has its type rather in some tremendous forensic battle, where the giants of the law dispute and contend, each intent on the victory.[7]

The clamorous accusations, subtle insinuations, and infernal malignity illustrate graphically the day-to-day tactics of hell's forces. Though many of Satan's accusations might have been true in the past, Christ has paid for them, and now the saints stand justified and forgiven. "They overcame him (Satan) because of the blood of the Lamb, and because of the word of their testimony; and they loved not their life even unto death" (12:11). Every accusation of Satan is drowned in the blood of the Lamb. The war of words is on, and the great voice from heaven thunders, "Rejoice, O heavens, and ye that dwell in them; woe for the earth and for the sea, because the Devil is gone down unto you, having great wrath, knowing that he hath but a short time" (12:12).[8] Seven years is a short time compared to the thousand years Satan will be chained in the abyss (20:1-3), so he makes the most of his limited time to pursue his program of persecution.

THE SEED OF THE WOMAN (12:13-17)

Their Identity

Since the woman is called a "sign," her seed (*spérma,*

7/Seiss, *op. cit.,* p. 309.
8/See page 113.

neuter singular) should also be interpreted figuratively. (*Spérma* is another illustration of a neuter singular noun used in a collective sense.) The woman and her seed, representing the visible and invisible church, are now persecuted intensely by the Dragon.

Their Persecution

The visible church during the Tribulation is largely luke-warm, but the intense persecution does one of two things for these individuals: it either brings them to full repentance and fellowship with God or it causes them to fall away and receive the mark of the Beast (13:16, 17). Since it will cost too much to profess Christ falsely, the persecution will rid the visible church of hypocrites. According to the picture in the fifth seal, many will suffer martyrdom for their faith in Christ and many others will be translated out of the Tribulation near the middle of the seven-year period (Revelation 7).

Their Food

Just how the sun-clothed woman and her seed will be nourished in the wilderness is not clear, but the same God who fed Israel in the wilderness, Elijah by the brook, and 5000 people during Christ's earthly ministry will still be in control of the universe! The mother and son will be nourished 1260 days (12:6) or 3½ years (12:14). This would take them halfway through the Tribulation period, and up to the time the Antichrist breaks his covenant with the Jews.[9]

Their Refuge

Even though the Old Serpent casts out of his mouth water as a river to swallow up the woman and her seed, the earth will help by opening up her mouth, as in the days of Korah.[10] The woman will be given "the two wings of the great eagle, that she might fly into the wilderness" for refuge (12:14). This figure is clarified by the words of Moses: "As an eagle

9/Dan. 9:27.
10/Num. 16:31-33.

that stirreth up her nest, that fluttereth over her young, he spread abroad his wings, he took them, he bare them on his pinions. Jehovah alone did lead him" (Deut. 32:11, 12). The woman's place of refuge is probably the same Sinai wilderness where God led the children of Israel. However, not all of the woman's seed will find refuge, for the Dragon "went away to make war with the rest of her seed, that keep the commandments of God[11] and hold the testimony of Jesus" (12:17). The persecution of the saints during the Great Tribulation will be worldwide, and the result will be martyrdom in a great many cases.

SUMMARY

Though the conflict between God and Satan is fierce, have you noticed that the opposing forces are headed up by *Michael* and Satan? The Christ of the conflict is so powerful that his representative, Michael, can handle things at this point, leaving Christ free to meet his saints in the air. Satan is cast out of the aerial regions to the earth so that the man-child overcomers can pass through the air to meet their blessed Lord.[12]

We have seen the visible church (represented by the sun-clothed woman), the invisible church (represented by the man-child), Satan's opposition to the translation of the man-child overcomers, the victory of Michael and his angels which permitted this translation, God's protection of the woman in the wilderness, Satan's persecution of some of the woman's seed, and Satan's expulsion from the aerial regions to the earth.

We have also noticed that Revelation 12 is an example

---

[11]/"Of God" and "of Jesus" are both subjective genitives, showing that God gave the commandments and that Jesus produced the testimony. According to Granville Sharp's rule (Dana and Mantey, *A Manual Grammar of the Greek New Testament,* p. 147), those who hold the testimony of Jesus are the same as those who keep the commandments of God—not two separate groups of Jews and Gentiles. All of this shows marvelous unity not only between the Father and the Son but also between the commandments which are given by the Father and the testimony borne by Jesus in the Revelation.
[12]/1 Thess. 4:16, 17.

of John's overlapping chronology, and that it provides further details of the events of Chapter 4. These events gather around five of the seven personages in this segment—the sun-clothed woman, the red Dragon, the male child, Michael, and the seed of the woman. We will examine the other two personages when we study Revelation 13.

11

CHRIST REAPS IN THE CONFLICT

Revelation 13, 14

INSTRUCTIONS FOR STUDYING REVELATION 13 AND 14

Read Jude 1-7 as a devotional approach to these chapters. Thank God for being one of the called. Then study Revelation 13 and 14, using all the study methods you have learned so far. Label and group the paragraphs in light of the preceding chapters. Then use the following questions to stimulate further observations.

1. What is the chronological position of Chapters 13 and 14?
2. Describe the Beasts. What is their source? What can they do?
3. Compare the trinity of evil with the trinity of good.
4. Compare the Beasts of Revelation with those of Daniel 7 and 8.
5. What is the significance of the sea in 13:1?
6. What is the contextual significance of the time element in 13:5?
7. Who are the saints in 13:7? Compare them with the saints in 6:9; 7:9; 12:7-17.
8. What is the full significance of 13:8?

9. Contrast 13:14 with Luke 23:33. Can you now identify the first Beast?

10. How does Chapter 14 illustrate the law of recurrence?

11. How do the members of the firstfruits company reach their destination?

12. Why would an angel proclaim the gospel? What gospel is this?

13. What other designations are used in the New Testament for the gospel?

14. Compare 14:12 with 12:17 and 13:10.

15. How many angels appear in Chapter 14? Can you group them? What is their responsibility?

16. Identify the harvests in Chapter 14. Who are the reapers?

17. Take a good look at 14:20. What do you see?

18. In which part of the Great Tribulation do you place Chapters 13 and 14? Why?

NOTES ON REVELATION 13, 14

THE THREE EVIL PERSONAGES (13:1-18)

The Christ who prepared for the conflict in Revelation 4 and 5, who opened the conflict in Chapter 6, who rescued his chosen groups in Chapter 7, who effected the six trumpet judgments in Chapters 8 and 9, who precipitated the conflict in Chapters 10 and 11, and who delivered the man-child out of the conflict in Chapter 12 now reaps another harvest of overcomers in Chapters 13 and 14.

Revelation 12, 13, and 14 constitute a segment of the book which we might call *The Seven Personages*. The first five appear in Chapter 12: the sun-clothed woman, the red Dragon, the male child, Michael, and the seed of the woman. These were identified as the visible church, the Devil, the invisible church, the archangel Michael, and the tribulation saints. The last two personages, the Beast out of the sea and the Beast out of the earth, are described in Chapter 13.

The Great Red Dragon (13:1)

Revelation 13 is really a continuation of Chapter 12, and the "he" of verse 1 refers to the great red Dragon of 12:16.[1] Keep in mind that Revelation 12, 13, and 14 take the reader through most, if not all, of the seven-year Tribulation period. Chapter 12 begins with the rapture of the male child and takes us through the first 1260 days of this worldwide trial (verses 6, 14). Chapters 13 and 14 take us through the next 42 months (13:5) and depict the power of the unholy "trinity of evil." Chapter 14 shows how 144,000 Jewish "firstfruits" escape the last part of the last half of the Great Tribulation. Chapter 14 then closes with a short account of the military campaign of the seven-year period, commonly known as the War of Armageddon.

The great red Dragon of 13:1 is the source of all the power displayed by the two Beasts of this chapter. Even though Satan works behind the scenes, let us never forget that his main goal is to oppose God and his saints in every way he can.

The Beast out of the Sea (13:1-10)

His source

The source of the first wild Beast (*thērion*, 13:1) is the sea and the abyss (17:8).[2] Since the Dragon stands on the sand of the sea at the point where land and sea meet, he depicts a usurper claiming the right to rule the land and the sea. In reality all the power and authority he has assumed belong to Christ alone. Remember that in 10:5 John saw a Personage "standing upon the sea and upon the earth" with his right hand lifted to heaven and with the declaration that there would be no delay in finishing the mystery of God. This "strong angel" was identified as "the Angel of Jehovah,"

---

[1]/The Greek text indicates that 13:1 should really be 12:18, and that the verb *estáthē* is the textual support for "he stood." So 13:1 refers to the Dragon—not John. This interpretation furnishes the proper bridge between Chapters 12 and 13.

[2]/*Thērion* is used 46 times in the N.T., and 38 of these are in Revelation. In 13:1, he is defined as the wild beast of prey. Contrast him with the tame beast of burden (*ktēnos*) in Luke 10:34.

Christ himself. At this point in Chapter 13 the Dragon is reminded that he has only 3½ years left, and John sees the usurper preparing his representatives for an all-out attack. "The sea. and the earth" are equivalent to "the whole world," so the origin of both these Beasts is fallen mankind. Satan has selected these two individuals to be indwelt by demon spirits from the abyss.

His description

The Beast out of the sea has seven blasphemous heads and ten horns with diadems. The Dragon also has ten horns, but his seven diadems are on his seven heads rather than on his horns (12:3). The number seven symbolizes God's dealing with men (3 plus 4), and the crowned usurper, the Dragon, appropriates this number and delegates his power to a pseudo-royal Beast. Though the Beast's *heads* are not crowned (13:1), the ten diadems on his *horns* signify the division and delegation of the Dragon's power.

The Beast's further description in verse 2 shows him to be basically like a leopard, but with feet like a bear and a mouth like a lion. His power comes from the Dragon and his throne. All this contrasts diabolically with the throne of the heavenly Trinity in Revelation 4. The reverse sequence of the animals as described in Daniel 7 shows this Beast out of the sea to be a combination of every bestial power—in other words, the culmination of Babylonian political confusion.

His identity

The whole evil system of lawlessness has now finally been headed up in the Man of Sin, whom John calls the Antichrist.[3] Daniel calls him the little horn, the Prince, and the wilful king.[4] Paul calls him the Man of Sin, the son of perdition, the lawless one, and the culmination of the mystery of lawlessness.[5] Matthew and Mark call him the abomination of desolation.[6]

That the Beast out of the sea is an impersonation of Christ

3/1 John 2:18, 22; 4:3.
4/Dan. 7, 8, 9, 11.
5/2 Thess. 2:3-8.
6/Matt. 24:15; Mark 13:14.

is verified by 13:3—"I saw one of his heads as though it had been smitten unto death; and his death-stroke was healed, and the whole earth wondered (*thaumázō*) after the beast." The sacred head of Christ was also wounded to death, and the Beast's apparent death and resurrection causes the whole earth to wonder after him and to worship both him and the Dragon. The adoration of the earth-dwellers is expressed in the words, "Who is like unto the beast, and who is able to war with him?" (13:4). What a diabolical deception!

His words

The delegated power from the Dragon enables the first Beast to keep speaking[7] great things and blasphemous words against God—against his name, against his tabernacle, and against the saints who tabernacle in the heavens. This authority to "continue" and to blaspheme (*poiēsai* and *blasphēmē'sai*) is stretched out over a 42-month period, and the Beast's authority is worldwide (13:7). Tribulation saints will be the special targets of his warfare, and he will be allowed to overcome many of them. All earth-dwellers will worship him, and "these are those whose names have not been written in the book of life of the Lamb, the One who has been slain from the world's foundation."[8]

So the Beast represents world power during the last half of the Great Tribulation. Daniel's beasts are successive empires, but John's beasts are the culmination of all world kingdoms under the Antichrist. He is the consummate antagonist of everything divine and the archenemy of all the saints. But powerful as Satan may appear to be, Christ will ultimately triumph in the conflict!

Christ's admonition

The sevenfold admonition which appeared in the letters to the seven churches now appears once again: "If any man hath an ear, let him hear" (13:9). But this time John adds,

---

[7]/*Laloún* is a durative present infinitive, and it shows the continuous action of the Beast.

[8]/This translation of 13:8 follows the word order of the Greek sentence, and shows the timelessness of the Cross and its effectiveness in the salvation of all Old Testament saints.

"If any man is for captivity (*aichmalōsía*),[9] into captivity he goeth" (verse 10). In other words, whoever renders himself an earth-dweller must go to hell. To worship the Beast is to suffer eternal punishment with no chance of reprieve. The statement "If any man shall kill with the sword, with the sword must he be killed" (13:10) means that whoever slays the saints must suffer God's just retribution. This is not a caution against legitimate civil defense but a warning against persecuting the saints. During the Great Tribulation the saints must exercise patience (*hupomonē,* endurance, 13:10) and faith. Matthew 24:13 promises, "He that endureth to the end, the same shall be saved." This promise was not given primarily to believers of the church age, but to those saints who must face the Satanic pressures of the Great Tribulation.

The Beast out of the Earth (13:11-18)

His description

The Beast out of the earth (13:11) also originates from fallen mankind, and his power, which comes from the Dragon, is represented by only two horns. His resemblance to the Lamb gives him an innocent, harmless appearance, but his dragon-like voice betrays him, for he is the counterfeit of the Holy Spirit in Satan's blasphemous trinity of evil. In Revelation 20:10 he is called the false prophet.

His work

This false prophet is the willing agent of the first Beast, the Antichrist, and his delegated power comes from Satan (13:2, 12). So both the Antichrist and the false prophet receive their power from the same diabolical source. Just as the Holy Spirit directs worship to Christ, so the false prophet (the Beast out of the earth) directs worship to the Antichrist (the Beast out of the sea). Their direct connection with the supernatural spirit world (17:8) explains their ability to perform great signs or miracles.

This second Beast is able to call fire down from heaven and to perform other miracles which deceive earth-dwellers.

9/Cf. Eph. 4:8—the only other place where the word is used.

He even instigates worship of the first Beast by causing the Beast's image to live and speak. As in the days of Nebuchadnezzar,[10] all who do not worship the image of the Beast are killed. Though Nebuchadnezzar could not unify all world religions, the Antichrist and the false prophet will succeed in doing so. Everyone who rejects the mark of the beast will be prohibited from buying or selling (13:17). This sieve is small enough to catch everyone! But God has his seal too (7:2-11; 9:4), and Revelation 14 shows how the 144,000 sealed believers will be translated into the presence of the holy Trinity and the throne. The tribulation saints who remain on earth will suffer untold agony and death. The woman in Chapter 12 was promised nourishment in a safe wilderness site for the first half of the Great Tribulation, but what about now—the last half? Will the war of the Dragon against the rest of her seed (12:17) exterminate the last saint on earth? Hardly, for though many saints are slaughtered, Chapter 15 shows that some "come off victorious from the beast, and from his image, and from the number of his name" (15:2). Hallelujah!

Some Bible students do not believe that Satan can perform miracles, but the work of the Egyptian magicians of Exodus 7:11, 12 should correct this notion. It is well known that demon doctors in heathen countries today demonstrate miraculous powers in many ways. If Satan is a supernatural being, why should we doubt that he has supernatural powers? We might be justified in fearing him were it not for the fact that our God is almighty! "Greater is he that is in you than he that is in the world" (1 John 4:4).

John says that the Beast's number (666) is that of a man (13:18). Since the Beast will be worshipped, we may conclude that this present age will end with the worship of man instead of God. Dr. Ralph Earle says,

> Already this trend is gaining great impetus. By the beginning of the twentieth century, humanistic theology, denying the deity of Jesus and eliminating the supernatural from the Bible, had swept from Germany and Britain into America. Two world wars,

---

10/Dan. 3.

which gave every evidence of being apocalyptic judgments, saw a reaction in the form of neoorthodoxy. But this has been largely replaced by neoliberalism. The final fruit of all this is the "God is dead" movement, which sprang into the open in 1965. Having dismissed God from His universe, man is now worshipping himself. The stage is set for the worship of the beast.[11]

THE THREE HEAVENLY VISIONS (14:1-20)

Revelation 14 contains three heavenly visions, each introduced by the words "and I saw" (*kaì eídon*) (verses 1, 6, and 14). The first vision pictures 144,000 saints standing with the Lamb on Mount Zion and having his name and the name of his Father written in their foreheads.

The Translated Jews (14:1-5)

Their identity

The first of these three heavenly visions is that of the translated Jews. The likeness of this translated group to the 144,000 "sealed out of every tribe of the children of Israel" (7:4) can hardly be overlooked. They stand in contrast to the earth-dwellers of Chapter 13, those who received the mark of the Beast. These Israelites received the seal of God while still on earth, and now in heaven they have the name of God in their foreheads. In Revelation 7 they were on the earth during the first half of the Great Tribulation, but now they stand before the throne in heaven during the last half of the seven-year period. The implication is that God shortened the days of suffering for these elect[12] by translating them into his very presence. So we have seen groups of saints translated in Chapters 4, 7, 11, 12, and 14. This indicates that the rapture occurs in phases over a period of time.

Their song

The saints' victory over the Beast brings a glorious response

---

11/Earle, *op. cit.*, p. 578.
12/Matt. 24:22.

of worship—voices like many waters and great thunder, musicians playing on their harps, and the singing of a new song by the 144,000 redeemed Israelites standing before the throne, the living creatures, and the elders. And no one could learn that song except the 144,000 who had been purchased out of the earth. They were translated because they had followed after the Lamb with hearts prepared for worship. They are spiritual virgins, for they rejected the fornication of Beast-worship (Chapter 13). In their mouths is found no lie, for they spurned the deceptive, lying wonders of the false prophet. These saints are without blemish!

The Three Angels (14:6-13)

The first angel preaches

The second vision of Revelation 14 begins with an angel flying in mid-heaven and proclaiming the eternal gospel to all earth-dwellers—to every nation, tribe, tongue, and people. This is the fulfillment of Matthew 24:14—"And this gospel of the kingdom shall be preached in the whole world for a testimony unto all the nations; and then shall the end come." In spite of all that Satan can do, God in his mercy gives men still another chance to be saved. Because all gospel witness will have been banned by the Antichrist, God will use an angel as his messenger to proclaim the eternal gospel to the whole world. Neither the Dragon nor his two evil Beasts can turn off God's mid-heaven telecast! The activities of Satan are confined to the earth, and the only recourse of the trinity of evil is to blaspheme. Like an unrepentant criminal whose blasphemous activities are confined to his cell, the Dragon and his angels continue to malign the trinity of God, the holy angels, and all the heavenly host of the redeemed (13:6). Yet in spite of all this God's message pierces through the blackness in these words: "Fear God and give him glory, for the hour of his judgment is come; and worship him that made the heaven and the earth and sea and fountains of waters" (14:7).

The second angel announces

The proclamation of the gospel by the first angel seals the doom of religious Babylon, so the second angel follows with the words, "Fallen, fallen is Babylon the great, that hath made all nations to drink of the wine of the wrath of her fornication" (14:8).[13] The same gospel that saves some damns others! The fall of ecclesiastical Babylon occurs after the beginning of the second half of the Great Tribulation and is fully described in Chapter 17.

The third angel warns

The third angel in this second vision warns men against worshipping the Beast and receiving his mark. Everyone who denies God by accepting the mark of the Beast will drink of the undiluted wine of God's wrath (14:9, 10). There will be no mercy or chance of repentance—only torment with fire and brimstone in the presence of the Lamb, whose blood was shed to redeem men from such disgrace and anguish. The Lamb and the throne of heaven are central even in the torment of the damned.

Just how fire burns bodiless angels and the souls of men does not warrant speculation. All we know is that "human expressions arc used to represent what is really beyond our present powers of conception. This is also true with regard to heaven."[14] That heaven is an eternal place[15] and that the eternal fires of hell are real are the indisputable facts of divine revelation. Equally difficult to comprehend is the fact that this punishment will continue throughout the endless ages of eternity, for "they have no rest day and night." In contrast to this dreadful picture of torment, we see the patience of the saints who keep the commandments of God and the faith of Jesus. The beatitude of verse 13 is the complete opposite of the fate of Babylon and all her children (verses 8-11). Blessed are the martyrs who rest from their toils! This is the second beatitude in the Book of Revelation (cf. Rev. 1:3).

The Two Harvests (14:14-20)

The harvest of saints

The third vision in Revelation 14 is the complement to the

13/Cf. Jer. 25:15; 50:38; 51:7.
14/Lenski, *op. cit.*, p. 437.
15/John 14.

first two—the twofold harvest and the end of the Great Tribulation.[16] The first harvest in verses 14 through 16 is that of the saints, and it is reaped by the Son of Man. His position on the cloud and his golden crown identify him as Christ. On earth he wore the crown of thorns, but in heaven he wears the golden crown of Deity.[17] The angel who appears here with the words "Send forth thy sickle and reap" does not supervise the work of God, but merely gives the signal for action. By this signal all the angels are alerted, so that when Christ casts his sickle on the earth the angels finish the job of reaping. Verse 16 does not mean that Christ actually did the wielding of the sickle, but rather that "the earth was reaped" (passive voice) by Christ through the instrumentality of angels. Just as an architect "constructs" a building without driving a single nail, so Christ uses his angels as agents to reap the earth.

What is the harvest that is fully ripe or dried out? The church, the 144,000, and the martyrs of 14:13 have all gone to heaven, so who are these people? They are perhaps the last group of tribulation saints to be taken up before the coming of Christ to reign. Keep in mind that Chapters 13 through 16 record events in the last half of the Great Tribulation.[18]

The reaping instrument, the sickle, is mentioned only twelve times in the Bible, and seven of these occurrences are in Revelation 14. "Sharp" (*óxos*) appears seven times in Revelation—four times here and three in describing the two-edged sword which proceeds out of the Lord's mouth. All this indicates efficiency and perfection in reaping and judging.

The harvest of sinners

Two more angels appear for the second harvest. The temple angel carries a sharp sickle and the altar angel has power over fire. Then the altar angel signals the temple angel to reap the clusters of the vine of earth with his sickle. The earth's cup of iniquity is full, for the grapes are fully ripe. The sickle is cast into the earth[19] and the vintage of the earth is

---

16/Mark 4:29.
17/Cf. Heb. 2:9.
18/Cf. Matt. 24:31.
19/The active voice in the Greek is used here instead of the passive (as in verse 16), so it is the angel who does the actual work of reaping.

gathered. It is cast into the great winepress of the wrath of God, and the blood of the grapes is pressed out. The source of this judgment is the temple, showing that the judgment is an act of God's holiness. The sharpness of the sickle is emphasized by the repetition of the Greek article in verse 18, and the result of this great reaping is a river of blood 1600 stades long, or about 165 miles. What a picture of Armageddon! The details of this last great battle of the Great Tribulation will be described in later chapters, but it might be well to point out here that "Armageddon" is a Hebrew word meaning "the mountain of Megiddo."[20] Near this mountain in northern Palestine a plain extends from the Mediterranean Sea eastward. Napoleon called it the world's greatest natural battlefield. Add to this the "Valley of Jehoshaphat"[21] on the east, situated between Jerusalem and the Mount of Olives, and you have the battlefield of the second half of the Great Tribulation, when the king of the south (probably Egypt) and the king of the north (probably Russia) will push against the glorious land of Palestine.[22]

Current events in the Middle East show the imminence of such action. The Soviet Union has been sending pilots, fighter planes, and missiles to Egypt. Russian installations, airfields, infantry, tank training areas, and military workshops constitute an important part of Egypt's total military might. NATO analysts believe that the Middle East, and not Indochina, is Russia's preferred area for expansion.

Since the Antichrist will have made a covenant with the Jews at the beginning of the Great Tribulation, this whirlwind push of the kings of the north and south will be a direct thrust against him and his ten-kingdom confederacy. At this point God himself intervenes to destroy the invaders with his supernatural judgment of pestilence, hailstones, fire, and brimstone.[23] This will mark the end of Russian Communism, and the Antichrist will rule over the entire world. There will be one government, one religion, and one world dictator. The

---

[20]/Cf. Zech. 12:11; Rev. 16:12-16.
[21]/Joel 3:2, 12; Zech. 14:1-8. Cf. Isa. 34.
[22]/Dan. 11:40.
[23]/Ezek. 38:18-22.

Antichrist will then move into Palestine, the "navel of the earth,"[24] and will rule the whole world for approximately three years. Then Christ will take over.

SUMMARY

Revelation 13 and 14 complete the segment started in Chapter 12 by adding the last two of the seven personages—the Beast out of the sea and the Beast out of the earth—and by showing the three heavenly visions. The two Beasts added in Chapter 13, together with the Dragon, represent the trinity of evil—Satan, the Antichrist, and the false prophet. They are the counterpart of the trinity of God—Father, Son, and Holy Spirit.

The three heavenly visions of Revelation 14 include the 144,000 translated Israelites, the three angels who preach, announce, and warn, and the two harvests of saints and sinners.

This segment takes the reader from the beginning of the Great Tribulation to its very last harvests and the beginning of the campaign of Armageddon. It includes the overthrow of Russian Communism and the establishment of a one-man dictatorship. But in spite of the fierce opposition of the infernal trinity of evil, Christ proves that he is still in control by manifesting total victory in the conflict.

---

[24]/Ezek. 38:12, ASV margin.

12

CHRIST WARNS IN THE CONFLICT

Revelation 15, 16

INSTRUCTIONS FOR STUDYING REVELATION 15 AND 16

Read Jude 8-16 as your devotional approach, asking the Lord to give you the same faith for translation that Enoch had. Just as he escaped the judgment of the Flood, so you may "prevail to escape" (Luke 21:36) the "water as a river" (Rev. 12:15) which the Dragon will use to persecute the woman. Study Revelation 15 and 16 by every study method known to you, then use the following questions to stimulate further observations. Keep your chart up-to-date!

1. How are Chapters 15 and 16 related to each other? What law does this illustrate?
2. Is the temple of these chapters on earth or in heaven? Where has it been mentioned before?
3. Are these chapters parallel in time with any previous chapter or chapters? What are the evidences for your answer?
4. How does the key word "sign" help you to interpret these chapters? What other key word appears?
5. Who are the victors of 15:2? Over what have they been victorious?

6. Can you identify these victors with any previously-mentioned group?

7. What are the source, the character, and the purpose of the bowls?

8. Are the bowl judgments exclusive or culminative? Explain.

9. What is the song of the victors? Compare Deuteronomy 32.

10. Compare Revelation 16:13-16 with 14:17-20. What do you see?

11. Compare 16:15 with 3:3. Correlate the information.

12. What law does 16:19 illustrate? How is this significant?

13. Compare the endings of Chapters 11 and 16. Then read Haggai 2:6, 7 and Zechariah 14:14. What do you see?

NOTES ON REVELATION 15, 16

GOD'S WRATH (15:1)

The Christ who prepared for the conflict in Revelation 4 and 5, who opened the conflict in Chapter 6, who rescued his chosen groups in Chapter 7, who effected six trumpet judgments in Chapters 8 and 9, who precipitated the conflict in Chapters 10 and 11, who delivered the man-child out of the conflict in Chapter 12, and who reaped still another harvest in Chapters 13 and 14 now gives his last warnings in the conflict by pouring out the seven bowls of judgment. Revelation 14 contains the last warning of *words* (14:9-12) while Chapters 15 and 16 contain the final warnings of *deeds*. These two chapters really form a single unit because Chapter 15 provides the setting for the events of Chapter 16.

Revelation 15:1 summarizes the full description in Chapter 16 of the seven golden bowls of the wrath of God. Since these seven last plagues are called a "sign" (*sēmeíon*), we should interpret them figuratively. So far John has seen three groups of signs. The first of these was the woman, her child, and her seed, representing the visible church, the invisible church, and the tribulation saints. The second group of signs was the Dragon and his two wild Beasts, representing the trinity of evil known as the Devil, the Antichrist, and the false prophet. Here in Chapter 15 John sees his third group of signs, described as "great and marvelous" (*thaumastón*). This group contains the seven last plagues or bowls, which finish the wrath of God. So Christ gives his last warnings in the conflict by smiting the entire antichristian establishment with seven great blows.

God's tribulation wrath began at the opening of the first seal in Revelation 6, and the seventh seal proved to be the source of the seven trumpet judgments of Chapter 8. We saw in Chapter 10 that the seventh trumpet would cover a period of time during which the mystery of God would be finished. More details about this period of time were shown in the last part of Chapter 11: the reign of Christ, the worship of the twenty-four elders, the wrath of the nations, the judgment of the dead, and the rewards of the slaves. Chapters 15 and 16 add further details to this period when the mystery of God is finished, for the third series of judgments take the viewer to the end of the Great Tribulation. These judgments were all contained in the seven-sealed book, the title deed to the earth. The last of the seven seals revealed the seven trumpets, and the last trumpet contained the seven bowls which are now to be poured out upon earth-dwellers. "In them is finished the wrath of God" (15:1).

GOD'S VICTORS (15:2-4)

In contrast to the wrath of God, which climaxes these chapters, John sees a company of God's victors standing on the transparent sea and holding the harps of God. "They sing the song of Moses the servant of God, and the song of the Lamb, saying,

Great and marvelous are thy works, O Lord God, the Almighty;
Righteous and true are thy ways, thou King of the ages.

Who shall not fear, O Lord, and glorify thy name?
   For thou only art holy;
For all the nations shall come and worship before thee;
   For thy righteous acts have been made manifest (15:3, 4).

     The mention of the sea, of the song of the Lamb, of the four living creatures, and of the glory of God in verses 2 through 8 reminds us that the setting here is the same as in Chapter 4. An interesting point of difference is that this transparent sea has been mingled with fire, emphasizing the punitive aspect of the throne of the Father and of the Lamb. Because of this judgmental aspect of the Great Tribulation on the whole antichristian kingdom and because of the purgative effect of the fires of this period, a company of victors stands on the transparent sea. They have "come off victorious" from the Beast, from his image, and from the number of his name.

     Just as Moses led Israel safely out of Egypt and the crushing hand of Pharaoh, so the Lamb delivers these tribulation saints out of the world and the oppression of the Antichrist. God's righteousness is manifested in judgment as much as in salvation (15:2-4), and the wording of the victors' song shows that the whole universe will finally learn to fear God, though unwillingly in the case of some creatures (cf. Phil. 2:9-11).

GOD'S TEMPLE (15:5-8)

     The temple in heaven is opened immediately after the singing of the marvelous ode (15:5). Though the last verse of Revelation 11 provided John with his first glimpse of this opened temple, he does not describe the details until now.

     The source of the seven last plagues is the sanctuary of the holy of holies, the very presence of God. The angels to whom the plagues were committed are clothed with pure, brilliant linen and are girded about the breasts with golden girdles. The linen[1] is a symbol of righteous acts (cf. 19:8),

---

[1]/Nestle's Greek text and the Bible Societies' Greek New Testament prefer *linon* (linen) instead of *lithon* (stone), and it does fit the context better than "stone." See 15:6, ASV, margin.

and the gold shows that God is the real source of these divine judgments (1:13). The God of mercy must also be the God of justice. He is making this earth a fit place for his reign of righteousness. One of the four living creatures (who represent the earthly agents of God's providence) gives these seven heavenly agents the golden bowls after they come out of the sanctuary with the seven plagues. The plagues fill the bowls to the brim, and the long-restrained anger of God is now suddenly executed in full. This is of course not the final judgment at the end of the Millennium but the final judgment of the Great Tribulation period, which closes this age of grace.

The result of equipping the seven angels with the bowl judgments is similar to what Moses experienced when he completed the tabernacle in the wilderness and what Isaiah experienced when he saw the Lord in the temple: an overwhelming manifestation of God's presence, described as a cloud and as smoke. "None was able to enter into the temple till the seven plagues of the seven angels should be finished" (15:8).

GOD'S JUDGMENTS (16:1-21)

Again a great voice is heard from heaven, and this time the command is to pour out the seven bowls of the wrath of God. The bowl plagues are both cumulative and culminative, for in verse 11 the boils of the first plague are still active during the fifth plague. These three series of judgments culminate in an overwhelming climax, for the final effects of the seals, the trumpets, and the bowls all converge on the earth-dwellers at the same time.

Grievous Sore (16:2)

The first angel pours his bowl into the earth, producing a foul and angry abscess upon all the worshipers of the Beast. But this plague, like some of the plagues of Egypt,[2] does not touch the tribulation saints who are still on the earth.

2/Exod. 9:8-12.

Bloody Sea (16:3)

The second bowl is poured out into the sea, producing stinking blood instead of the normal sparkling water. Every living being in the sea dies—not just one-third, as in the second trumpet (8:8), but everything! The stench of the sea and the putrefaction of their ulcers makes life almost unbearable for the worshipers of the Beast.

Bloody Rivers (16:4-7)

It was not enough to pollute the sea, so the third angel pours out his bowl into the rivers and fountains of waters (cf. 8:10), and they too become blood. The conversion of the sea into blood did not cut off drinking water, but now to the consternation of the earth-dwellers every source of fresh water pours forth only decaying blood.

Then the angel of the waters utters a statement about God's righteousness in retribution: "Righteous art thou, who art and who wast, thou holy One" (16:5).[3] Why the "holy One" instead of the "coming One," as in 4:8? Because Christ came *before* the Great Tribulation began (11:17). The response of the angel who came out of the altar (14:18) is, "Yea, O Lord God, the Almighty, true and righteous are thy judgments" (16:7). Again we note that God's righteousness is manifested as much in judgment as in mercy. These two responses indicate the end of the first set of judgments, for the bowl judgments are divided into groups of three and four.

Scorching Sun (16:8, 9)

The fourth bowl is poured out upon the sun. The change of the preposition from "into" to "upon" is another indication that the judgments are divided into groups of three and four. The first three are confined to the earth and are physical, but the next four affect heavenly bodies and the spirit world.[4]

---

[3]/See page 107. The imminence of Christ's second advent is emphasized by the present tense of *érchomai* in 1:4, 7, 8; 3:11; 4:8. The lack of this emphasis in the chapters describing the Great Tribulation argues for his coming prior to this time.

[4]/See pages 95, 96.

The sun that gave warmth and light to cheer the life of man-kind now scorches men with a kind of hell on earth. But do they now repent? No, they still reveal their stubborn opposition to God by blaspheming the name of their Maker.

Unbearable Pains (16:10, 11)

The fifth angel pours his bowl upon the throne of the Beast, resulting in darkness and excruciating pain. The imperfect tense indicates that the sufferers keep gnawing their tongues, possibly because in the total darkness they cannot see to treat their third degree burns and ulcerating sores. But instead of repenting at this point, they continue to blaspheme the God of heaven.

Demon Spirits (16:12-15)

The sixth bowl is poured upon the great Euphrates River (cf. 9:14). The water immediately evaporates, and the riverbed becomes a highway for the invasion of the kings of the east. Spirits of demons are then released from the mouths of the trinity of evil to work signs, to speak blasphemy, and to gather the kings of the earth together to fight in the campaign of the great day of God the Almighty. This campaign will eventually culminate in the Battle of Armageddon.

The kings of the east (16:12) may be identified as a fourth world power at the end time, along with the king of the south (Egypt), the king of the north (Russia), and the western coalition of the ten kingdoms headed up by the Antichrist. The Antichrist will relieve world tension by settling the Arab-Israeli dispute and drawing up his seven-year covenant with the Jews. Then, when he sees Russian Communism destroyed by the judgment of God, he will assume world dictatorship. "But tidings out of the east and out of the north shall trouble him" (Dan. 11:44; cf. Rev. 16:12). These kings of the east and north are probably a confederacy of Oriental or Asiatic nations from beyond the Euphrates River. The Antichrist will then "go forth with great fury to destroy and utterly sweep away" (Dan. 11:44) these invading hosts and plant his palace between the Dead Sea and the Mediterranean Sea. The consummation of this campaign is described in Revelation 19.

But now there is a brief intermission. Christ interrupts his sequence of revelations for a spot announcement. Though the proclamation might seem to be an interruption, it turns out to be a timely warning to everyone who is wise enough to read the Book of Revelation. The very fact that this announcement seems out of context is significant, for today's reader of Revelation seems out of step by secular standards, though he is actually preparing himself for a whole series of future events which could begin at any moment. "Behold, I come as a thief. Blessed is he that watcheth and keepeth his garments, lest he walk naked and they see his shame" (16:15).[5] Joseph Rabinovitch, a converted rabbi, was deeply moved as he encountered this passage.

> My heart was thrilled with the picture which is revealed. I knew so well what it meant. After the captain of the temple had posted the guards for the nightwatch, he would go at irregular intervals to inspect them. It might happen that one had fallen asleep. In such a case the captain simply stooped and gently pulled from beneath him his outer garment. Then, in the morning, the question, "Where is your garment?" removed all possibility of excuse. The culprit walked naked, and his shame was manifest.[6]

Great Hail (16:16-21)

When the seventh bowl is poured out upon the air, a great voice out of the holy of holies from the throne says, "It is done" (16:17; cf. 21:6). The climax is upon us. We are near the beginning of the seven dooms which mark the end of the Great Tribulation. The lightning, the voices, the earthquake, and the great hail show that Chapters 15 and 16 end at the same point of time as Chapter 11. The difference in the accounts is that more details are given here.

5/Cf. Matt. 24:43; Luke 12:39; 1 Thess. 5:2, 4; 2 Pet. 3:10; Rev. 3:3.
6/*The Alliance Weekly* (September 18, 1943), p. 594.

The fall of ecclesiastical Babylon announced in Revelation 14:8 is fully described in Chapter 17. The fall of commercial and political Babylon announced here (16:19) is fully described in Chapter 18. Babylon represents the whole antichristian world empire, and this empire is divided into three parts. So great is the earthquake that every island sinks into the oceans and all the mountains are leveled. Great hailstones weighing from sixty to one hundred pounds each rain down upon mankind. But once more John notes that men continue to blaspheme God because of the greatness of the suffering. The people who refused to repent under grace now blaspheme under judgment! Yet God grants them still another opportunity to be saved.

SUMMARY

In this whole section dealing with Christ in the conflict (Chapters 4—16), we have seen the Great Tribulation from two overlapping vantage points. Beginning with the rapture of the overcomers in Chapters 4 and 12 and continuing through the three series of judgments—the seals, the trumpets, and the bowls—we have seen Christ as the Master of the conflict. The composite picture of Christ's consummation in Chapter 11 was enlarged in the overlapping Chapters 13, 14, 15, and 16. The fall of ecclesiastical and political Babylon in Chapters 17 and 18 will highlight events that were not detailed in Chapters 14 and 16. The events of all these chapters (11, 13, 14, 15, 16, 17, and 18) fall within the last half of the Great Tribulation period. In the vision of Chapters 17 through 20 we shall see that the Christ of conflict becomes the Christ of conquest. Hallelujah!

PART FOUR

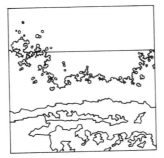

CHRIST
IN THE CONQUEST

13

CHRIST DESTROYS IN THE CONQUEST

Revelation 17, 18

Read Jude 14-23 as your devotional approach, and continue to build yourself up on your most holy faith. Pray in the Holy Spirit, keep yourself in the love of God, and wait for the mercy of our Lord Jesus Christ unto eternal life. Study Revelation 17 and 18, then relate these two chapters to each other and to the previous chapters. Use the following questions to stimulate further observations.

1. How do Revelation 17 and 18 fit into the chronology of the Book?
2. How do these chapters relate to Genesis 11?
3. Harmonize Revelation 17 and 18 with Isaiah 13:17-22 and Jeremiah 51:61, 62. What is the problem? What is the solution?
4. Does the angel's explanation in 17:8-18 help identify "Babylon"? Compare Daniel 2 and 7.
5. Can you name the seven world kingdoms, beginning with Egypt? Relate these to Revelation 17 and 18.
6. Compare Revelation 18:4 with 3:20.

STUDY PROJECT NUMBER 8

Thoroughly compare and contrast the women of Chapters 12 and 17, using horizontal or vertical columns. Now make significant observations and interpretations.

Are you working on your chart? Are you updating your other projects?

NOTES ON REVELATION 17, 18

THE FALL OF ECCLESIASTICAL BABYLON (17:1-18)

The first great showing of the Revelation of Jesus began in 1:9, and was seen from the Isle of Patmos. It included the vision of Christ in Chapter 1 and his central position among the churches in Chapters 2 and 3. The second great showing took place in heaven and spanned Chapters 4 through 16. It included the throne in heaven, the seven-sealed book, the seven trumpet judgments, the seven personages, and the seven bowl judgments—all showing Christ in the conflict. The third great showing begins in the wilderness and includes Chapters 17 through 20. It covers the seven dooms, the revelation of Jesus Christ from heaven, and the millennial reign of Christ on earth—all showing Christ in the conquest. In each of these three showings John is "in the Spirit."[1]

The key word which unlocks the correct interpretation of Revelation 17 and 18 is "mystery" (*mustērion,* 17:5, 7). This shows that Babylon should be interpreted figuratively. Since Isaiah and Jeremiah indicated that the city of Babylon would not be rebuilt,[2] the Babylon of Revelation 17 and 18 must mean something more than the literal city. What then does it mean?

The fall of Babylon is announced in Revelation 14, and there the emphasis is on ecclesiastical Babylon, the city that induces "all the nations to drink of the wine of the wrath of

---

[1]/Rev. 1:10; 4:2; 17:3. Cf. 21:10.
[2]/Isa. 13:19-22; Jer. 50:39.

her fornication" (14:8; 17:2). Though the fall of Babylon coincides chronologically with Chapter 14, the full description of this catastrophe is recorded here in Chapter 17. In other words, the overthrow of ecclesiastical Babylon by the first Beast or Antichrist will occur shortly after the middle of the Great Tribulation. The Antichrist then becomes the culmination of the whole Babylonish system of worship. Daniel 9, Matthew 24, and Mark 13 call him "the abomination of desolation."

The Mother of Harlots (17:1-6a)

The doom of ecclesiastical Babylon, the mother of harlots, is introduced by one of the seven angels with the seven bowls. He carries John to the vantage point of a wilderness, where he can show him the judgment (*kríma*) of the great harlot. *Kríma* does not signify the *act of judging* but the *result of the judgment* that has already taken place. This implies not only that the fall of Babylon has occurred in Chapter 14 but also that there is a very close relationship between the seven bowl judgments and the seven dooms. In fact, the seventh bowl includes the doom of Babylon (16:19).

The great whore is never called an "adulteress" (*moichalís*), for she was never the bride or wife of the Lamb; she was never anything but a whore. The kings of the earth had committed fornication with her, and the earth-dwellers had been drunk with the wine of her fornication.

John sees her sitting on many waters, and the angel interprets these waters to be peoples, multitudes, nations, and tongues (17:15; cf. 13:7). She exercises a well-established rule over the restless multitudes. John also sees her sitting on a scarlet-colored Beast. Scarlet is the color of sin[3] and is the opposite of white, the color of righteousness (6:11; 7:14). The Beast's scarlet color, seven heads, ten horns, and hellish origin (cf. 17:8) identify him with the Antichrist of Revelation 13. This in turn helps identify the woman. She is the counterpart of the sun-clothed woman of Chapter 12 and of the bride of 21:9. When John first sees the harlot he wonders

---

3/Isa. 1:18.

with great astonishment. When the Beast first displayed himself in Chapter 13 the whole earth wondered in admiration, but here John is perplexed. Could this possibly be the same woman that he saw in Chapter 12? Could the woman who delivered the man-child have degenerated into this mother of harlots?[4] At this point the angel explains the mystery, and John is relieved (17:7). The following contrasts should help in identifying this woman.

The Woman of Chapter 12	*The Woman of Chapter 17*
1. The travailing mother (12:2).	1. The abominable fornicator (17:1, 2, 4, 5, 15, 16).
2. The mother of the man-child (12:5).	2. The mother of harlots (17:5).
3. Produces masculine nobility (12:5).	3. Produces effeminate impurity (17:2, 4, 5, 16).
4. The mystery of God (10:7).	4. The mystery of Babylon (17:5, 7).
5. Standing on the moon (12:1).	5. Sitting on the Beast (17:3).
6. Arrayed with the sun (12:1).	6. Arrayed in purple and scarlet (17:4).
7. Crowned with twelve stars (12:1).	7. Decked with gold, precious stones, and pearls (17:4).
8. Nourished in the wilderness by God (12:14).	8. Drunken with the blood of saints and martyrs (17:6).
9. Fled to the wilderness (12:6, 14).	9. Viewed from the wilderness (17:1, 3).
10. Seen in heaven (12:1).	10. Seen on earth (17:2).
11. Opposed by the Dragon (12:4, 13, 15, 17).	11. Opposed by the ten kings (17:16).
12. Supported by celestial wings (12:14).	12. Carried by bestial power (17:3).

4/Cf. Isa. 1:21.

13. Protected by God (12: 9, 10, 14, 16).

13. Destroyed by the ten kings (17:16).

14. Symbol of the visible church which Christ preserved (12:14).

14. Symbol of the pseudo-church which the Antichrist destroys (17:16).

15. Inclusive of the people of God of all ages, beginning with righteous Abel and including the last saint saved during the Great Tribulation.

15. Inclusive of the whole Babylonish system of religious confusion which begins at the Tower of Babel and continues through more than half of the Great Tribulation.

16. Prophetically, the sun-clothed woman represents the visible and invisible church at the time of the first "catching up" and for most of the Great Tribulation thereafter. See pages 111-119.

16. Prophetically, the great harlot represents the culmination of the whole Babylonish religious system of confusion and deception, covering every form of false worship, and including apostate Protestantism and Roman Catholicism.

There are four reasons for including the Roman Catholic Church. First, she practices the mother-child cult of idolatry.[5] Second, she has been drunken with the blood of martyrs.[6] Third, many of her priests and nuns are guilty of fornication.[7] Fourth, the fear and superstition of the people have made her the wealthiest church system on earth.[8]

A significant feature of the present religious picture is the rise of the Vatican's power. In 1961 in New Delhi the World Council of Churches' Third Assembly not only underestimated the gap between Christianity and non-Christian religions, but admitted four additional Orthodox Churches,

[5]/Read Pentecost, *op. cit.,* Chapter 12.
[6]/Lester F. Sumrall, *Roman Catholicism Slays* (Grand Rapids: Zondervan Publishing House, 1940), pp. 5-35.
[7]/*Ibid.,* pp. 40-45.
[8]/*Ibid.,* pp. 35-40.

thereby ending the predominately Protestant character of the WCC. Many of these sacramental-ritualistic Orthodox Churches were from behind the Iron Curtain. Moreover, most of the obstacles to approaching Roman Catholics for membership have been removed. President H. "Pitt" Van Dusen of Union Theological Seminary once noted that there can be no effective world ecumenicity until Roman Catholics are brought in.[9] So the stage is being set by both Roman Catholics and ecumenical Protestants for the unity of religions which Revelation calls "mystery, Babylon the Great, the mother of the harlots and of the abominations of the earth" (17:5). If these current events have any significance whatever, the coming of our Lord must be very near indeed!

The Wild Beast (17:6b-14)

The wild Beast which carries the mother of harlots turns out to be the same Beast out of the sea that we saw in Chapter 13—the Antichrist. But more details are added here in Chapter 17, as shown by the following comparisons.

Chapter 13	*Chapter 17*
1. The Beast out of the sea (13:1).	1. The Beast out of the abyss (17:8).
2. Like a leopard, bear, and lion (13:2).	2. Scarlet-colored by the blood of saints and martyrs (17:3, 6).
3. Names of blasphemy on his seven heads (13:1).	3. Full of the names of blasphemy (17:3).
4. Significance of seven heads not given (13:1).	4. The seven heads are seven mountains or kings on which the woman sits (17:9).
5. His ten horns have ten diadems (13:1).	5. His ten horns are ten kings with no kingdom, but with authority as kings with the Beast for one hour (17:12).

---

[9]/Carl F. H. Henry, "Diversity in Unity: Report on New Delhi," *Christianity Today,* Vol. 6, No. 6 (Dec. 22, 1961), pp. 267-271.

This figure of the wild Beast is apparently a synechdoche (the use of a part to represent the whole), for the picture encompasses both the Antichrist and his kingdom. This kingdom is "about to come" and represents the Roman Empire in its final form, the ten-kingdom confederacy. The interpretation of "was" and "is not" (17:8) presents a problem. "Was," the past aspect of the Beast's kingdom at the time of John's writing, probably represented the work of Satan as he entered Judas and combined Roman and Jewish powers to crucify the Lord of glory (cf. John 13:27; Psalm 2:1-3). This phase of the kingdom had terminated by the time John wrote Revelation, and the final aspect was "about to come."[10] The wild Beast's appearance out of the abyss (17:8) indicates the Satanic origin of the Antichrist and his kingdom.

The seven heads of the Beast picture seven mountains or kings (17:9, 10). Five have fallen, one is, and the other has not yet come. Some commentators have identified these seven heads with seven Roman emperors: Julius Caesar, Tiberius, Caligula, Claudius, and Nero, who ruled before John's time; Domitian of John's day, a Roman king who will "continue a little while" (17:10); and, finally, the Antichrist. Other commentators have identified the seven heads or mountains with the seven different governmental forms of the Roman Empire: kings, consuls, dictators, decemvirs, and military tribunals before John's day; the imperial form of government in John's day; a Satanic revival of the Roman Empire as in Revelation 13; and an eighth head, the little horn on the ten-horned Beast.

I personally prefer to identify these seven heads of the Beast as the seven world kingdoms from Egypt and Assyria on through Babylon, Medo-Persia, Greece, Rome, and the ten-kingdom confederacy at the end time. In John's day five had

---

10/Note that the expression "is about to come up out of the abyss" (17:8) is omitted in verse 11: "And the beast that was, and is not, is himself also an eighth." This omission implies that by the time the Beast becomes "an eighth," the prophecy of verse 8 will have been realized, for he will have already come. This phenomenon also occurs with reference to Christ's coming. The last reference to the One "who is to come" is in 4:8. The succeeding references omit this phrase (11:7; 16:5) because Christ has already come for his saints in Chapter 4.

fallen, one existed (Rome), and the other had not yet come. This coming ten-kingdom confederacy will be headed up by the Antichrist, who will continue "a little while"—namely, the seven years of the Great Tribulation. He is also labeled an eighth horn, even though he originates out of the original seven. The ten horns are the ten confederate kings or puppet rulers who receive their authority from the Antichrist (17: 12, 13). These kings will "war against the Lamb, and the Lamb shall overcome them, for he is Lord of lords and King of kings; and they also shall overcome that are with him, called and chosen and faithful" (17:14). This is the announcement of Christ's conquest of Revelation 19, when he will completely repossess the earth by overthrowing every foe. His overcomers will come "with him" (17:14) for this conquest because they were translated before the conflict began (4:1).

The Ten Kingdoms (17:15-18)

The same angel who announces the mystery of the mother of harlots and the wild Beast also tells John that the ten horns turn upon the great harlot in hatred, rendering her desolate and naked. Then they eat her flesh and burn her thoroughly with fire. This pictures the amazing destruction of ecclesiastical Babylon by the ten-kingdom confederacy headed by the Antichrist. This destruction will take place after the beginning of the second half of the Great Tribulation and will put an end to Roman Catholicism and apostate Protestantism.

What is this ten-kingdom confederacy? Some interpreters believe that the entire old Roman Empire will be revived politically and territorially, while others believe that the revival will be limited to the territory which was once under Roman domination. According to Daniel's interpretation of Nebuchadnezzar's dream image (Dan. 2:26-45) and according to Daniel's beast vision of world kingdoms (Dan. 7:15-27), the fourth Beast represents the old Roman Empire. This is the fourth kingdom after Babylon or the sixth kingdom after Egypt. The ten-kingdom confederacy is to arise at least territorially "out of this kingdom" of Rome, and it will comprise the seventh world kingdom.

What nations will be included in this confederacy? Daniel 8:23 hints at four of them. Following a discussion of the Grecian empire under Alexander the Great (the great horn) and the division of his kingdom among four generals, Daniel says, "And in the latter time of their kingdom, when the transgressors are come to the full, a king of fierce countenance, and understanding dark sentences, shall stand up." This would indicate that Greece, Egypt, Syria, and Turkey will appear in the end time under the Antichrist. Arthur Petrie suggests the following ten as the complete list:

1. Britain or perhaps the United States allied with Britain;
2. France enlarged to the Rhine River;
3. Spain and Portugal, the old "Hispania";
4. United Italy;
5. Austria;
6. Greece;
7. Egypt;
8. Syria and possibly Israel (which was one province with Syria in the old Roman Empire);
9. Turkey;
10. The Balkan States in union, including Bulgaria, Rumania, and Hungary.[11]

After the death of Alexander the Great, Macedonia and Greece fell to Cassander, Egypt to Ptolemy Soter, Syria and the East (Iraq and Iran) to Seleucus, and Thrace and Bithynia (mainly Turkey and Bulgaria of today) to Lysimachus. The implication of Daniel 8:23 is that the Antichrist will rise from one of these four sections of the world, and the current status of the Common Market shows that this prophecy of the ten-kingdom confederacy could be fulfilled in the very near future.

Will Russia ever control the world? Even though Soviet Russia has experienced phenomenal growth, she can never be

---

11/Arthur Petrie, *Behind the Berlin Crisis and the Signs of the End* (Seattle, Washington, Arthur Petrie), pp. 9, 10.

a *bona fide* world power. With all the expanse of Communism during the past fifty years, only about three percent of the people of the Soviet Union are actually Communists. Though this system with all its modern psychological techniques of brainwashing represents the control of the few over the masses, Russia can never be a dominant world power, for she is outside the territory of the old Roman Empire. Germany tried to rule the world and failed, and Russia will follow in her footsteps.[12] The prophecies of Daniel and Revelation show that God has given world sovereignty to only six empires so far— Egypt, Assyria, Babylonia, Medo-Persia, Greece, and Rome. Only two more are possible: the ten-kingdom confederacy headed up by the Antichrist and the millennial kingdom headed up by Christ.

When will this ten-kingdom confederacy assume its final form? Even though we can see this confederacy on the horizon now, the final federation of the nations will take place only in the Great Tribulation, and probably during the second half. We should therefore be looking for the coming of Christ rather than the final formation of the ten-kingdom confederacy. However, the present status of the Common Market alerts us to the imminence of our Lord's return and fills us with joyful expectation of this blessed event.

THE FALL OF POLITICAL BABYLON (18:1-24)

The fall of political and commercial Babylon which was announced in Revelation 16:19, 20 is fully described in Chapter 18. This Babylonish system of political confusion began at the Tower of Babel in Genesis 11 and has been characterized by "wars and rumors of wars"[13] from the earliest day until now.

The Fall of the Nations (18:1-3)

The final crash of all human government is called the fall of the nations here in Revelation 18:3. Since the word

---

12/See pages 131, 132, 139.
13/Matt. 24:6.

"mystery" is used of Babylon in this section (see 17:5), the term "Babylon" in Chapter 18 applies primarily to government rather than to a literal city. This system is the ten-kingdom confederacy headed up by the Antichrist, and the words "fallen, fallen" in 18:2 probably mean that all the cities of the earth will fall with the collapse of Babylon.

There has been an alarming change in commercial industry in the last hundred years. In the nineteenth century, businessmen and craftsmen operated in order to serve their communities, and their reward was the satisfaction of a job well done. But with the massive development of industry came a commercial psychology aimed at persuading the public to spend as much money as possible. Industry has practically deified materialism, and more and more people are becoming entangled in this web of idolatry. Such a way of life leaves no place for God, and this Satanically-induced philosophy paves the way for the Babylonian condition of the world under the Antichrist. And Christ will ultimately have to overthrow it all.

The Antichrist, who has reigned for seven years—3½ as the deceitful promoter of Israel's welfare and 3½ as the great wild Beast who subdued the whole world under his dictatorship —is now completely overcome by Christ in the conquest. The fall of political and commercial Babylon probably occurs three years after the fall of ecclesiastical Babylon, since the Antichrist carries on a program of enforced worship of himself during most of the last half of the Great Tribulation. The Beast destroys the great harlot as soon as he can, for he cannot tolerate a single rival.

The Call of God's People (18:4-8)

Before Babylon is actually destroyed, John hears another voice from heaven saying, "Come forth, my people, out of her, that ye have no fellowship with her sins, and that ye receive not her plagues" (18:4). God has always had some people on earth who belong to him because they have not "bowed their knee to Baal." Just how he has preserved these Tribulation saints is not clear (12:17), but many believers will refuse the mark of the Beast and will inhabit the millennial earth as soon as the Great Tribulation is over. Notice that the voice did not say "Come up hither," as in Revelation 4:1, but rather "Come forth, my people, out of her" (18:4). This is not *translation* but *preservation* in order to populate the millennial earth. It is possible that the angel of Revelation 18:1 is the Angel of Jehovah, or Christ. So this call to his people would refer primarily to the Jews, who will enjoy a most prominent position in the millennial earth.

The Weeping of Earth-Dwellers (18:9-19)

The doom of commercial and political Babylon does not mean the destruction of all unsaved people, for a world of earth-dwellers remains to weep over the loss of its commerce. "The kings of the earth, who committed fornication and lived wantonly with her, shall weep and wail over her when they look upon the smoke of her burning, standing afar off for the fear of her torment, saying, Woe, woe, the great city, Babylon, the strong city! For in one hour is thy judgment come" (18:9, 10).

The merchants will also weep and mourn over the collapse of political and commercial Babylon, for no one will buy their merchandise anymore—their gold, silver, precious stones, pearls, fine linen, purple, silk, scarlet, thyine wood, ivory, brass, iron, marble, spices, incense, ointment, frankincense, wine, oil, fine flour, wheat, cattle, sheep, horses, chariots, slaves, and souls of men. The wheels of commerce that ran so smoothly have now stopped. Yet there is no true repentance for sins, but only remorse because their market is gone. What a warning for the modern spirit of commercialism which controls governments today! Commerce knows no god but gold, no law but profit. To the average businessman the Bible means nothing, Sunday means a holiday, and the end justifies the means. Even Christian businessmen today need to reappraise their values, to be sure they are not being swept away by this same spirit of commercialism.

Then the shipmasters, sailors, and mariners wail, "What city is like the great city? And they cast dust on their heads, and cried, saying, Woe, woe, the great city, wherein all that had their ships in the sea were made rich by reason of her costliness! For in one hour is she made desolate" (18:18, 19). Each of the three major groups of entrepreneurs cries "Woe, woe," giving rise to a triple voice of cataclysmic disaster.

The Rejoicing of God's Saints (18:20-24)

In contrast to the woeful laments of earth-dwellers, God's saints are exhorted to "Rejoice over her, thou heaven, and ye saints, and ye apostles, and ye prophets; for God hath judged your judgment on her" (18:20). For millenniums God's messengers have been proclaiming the justice of God and warning people of the judgment to come, but now these things are a reality. Those who have been burned at the stake and slain by the sword are now rejoicing because of the triumph of righteousness.

The suddenness of Babylon's fall is demonstrated by the strong angel who cast "a stone as it were a great millstone" into the sea with the words, "Thus with a mighty fall shall Babylon, the great city, be cast down, and shall be found no more at all" (18:21). Babylon's atheistic commercialism and religious persecution will have led to her total destruction.

SUMMARY

Revelation 17 provides a full description of the fall of ecclesiastical or religious Babylon. She is described as the mother of harlots, representing the culmination of the whole Babylonish religious system of confusion and deception. She includes every form of false worship, including Roman Catholicism and apostate Protestantism. Shortly after the first half of the Great Tribulation she is destroyed by the wild Beast on which she rides (the Antichrist) and by the ten-kingdom confederacy over which the Antichrist rules.

Revelation 18 describes the fall of political and commercial Babylon along with the final crash of all forms of human government. A group of God's people is called out just in time to be preserved for populating the millennial earth. The response of earth-dwellers to Babylon's fall is one of lament and dismay, but God's saints rejoice because of the justice and judgment of God upon sin. Christ's final conquest is described in Revelation 19 and 20.

14

CHRIST REIGNS IN THE CONQUEST

Revelation 19, 20

INSTRUCTIONS FOR STUDYING REVELATION 19 AND 20

Read Jude 24 and 25 as your devotional approach, praying to be kept from falling and to be presented without blemish before the presence of God's glory with rejoicing. Begin a chart on Revelation 19 and 20, revising it if necessary after completing your research. And remember to update your ribbon chart. Use the following questions to stimulate your personal study.

1. What is the relationship of Revelation 19 and 20 to Chapters 17 and 18?
2. How many "Hallelujahs" are there in Chapter 19? What is the cause for these expressions of praise? Who voices them?
3. How many times does the word "Hallelujah" occur in the Bible? How is this significant?
4. Who are the persons in Revelation 19? Relate them to previous references.
5. Compare and contrast the white horses and their riders in 6:2 and Chapter 19.
6. Does the second advent of Christ occur at a single

point of time or does it cover a period of time? Explain.

7. Who are the "armies which are in heaven" that followed the white horse and his rider in 19:14?

8. Who are the nations smitten by the King of kings and his armies?

9. Do the contents of Chapter 19 fit the title of the book? Where is the climax?

10. Compare 19:11-16 with 1:12-16. Have you kept Christ central throughout your study of Revelation? Be sure to also keep him central in your life!

11. Compare 20:1-3 with 9:1-11. Who is involved and what are the differences?

12. Do you interpret the "thousand years" of Revelation 20 figuratively or literally? Why?

13. How many times does "thousand years" occur in Chapter 20? How is this significant?

14. Are all the righteous people resurrected at the same time? Why would this be impossible?

15. What are the "books"? What is the "Book"? (20:12).

16. What is the second death (20:14)?

NOTES ON REVELATION 19, 20

THE REVELATION OF CHRIST (19:1-21)

Chapter 19 is the grand climax of the whole Book of Revelation. Here the Christ in conflict becomes the Christ of conquest. Here the Faithful Witness and the Firstborn of the Dead becomes the Ruler of the kings of the earth (1:5). Here the Christ who was found worthy to open the title deed to the earth (5:9) rides forth with the armies of heaven to put an end to the rule of the usurper. Here the Lamb slain from the foundation of the world (13:8, KJV) at last takes his place as King of kings and Lord of lords. This is truly *the revelation of Jesus Christ.*

The Four Hallelujahs (19:1-8)

The exhortation in Revelation 18:20 to rejoice over the destruction of Babylon is fulfilled by the universal response of the four hallelujahs (19:1-8). The basis for such rejoicing and worship is the judgment of Babylon described in Chapters 17 and 18.

The first hallelujah (19:1) is occasioned by the fall of religious or ecclesiastical Babylon, while the second hallelujah (19:3) is occasioned by the judgment on political or commercial Babylon. Both hallelujahs are voiced by a great multitude in heaven. The third hallelujah (19:4, 5) is uttered by the twenty-four elders and four living creatures, showing that the heavenly throne with all its personnel (see Revelation 4 and 5) is still the backdrop of a single great showing. The fourth hallelujah (19:6, 7) is expressed by all the preceding groups and sounds like the voice of a great multitude, the voice of many waters, and the voice of mighty thunders. The whole mighty chorus joins in worshiping the triune God.

Hallelujah! for the Lord our God, the Almighty, reigneth.
Let us rejoice and be exceeding glad,
And let us give the glory unto him;
For the marriage of the Lamb is come,
And his wife hath made herself ready.
And it was given unto her that she should array herself
In fine linen, bright and pure; for the fine linen is
The righteous acts of the saints (19:6-8).

"Hallelujah" is one of the very highest expressions of praise to God, and these four uses of the word in Revelation 19 are the only occurrences in the entire New Testament. It might have seemed that during the days of persecution and pressure God had forgotten justice and judgment. But not so, for God will correct everything in the end and will avenge his elect who cry to him day and night. The great harlot once had her day, but now she has been burned "utterly with fire" (17:16). The Beast and the false prophet had had their day too, but soon they are to be cast alive into the lake of fire. And the great red Dragon had had his day, but soon he is to be chained in the abyss for a thousand years.

The last five Psalms begin and end with "Hallelujah" (Praise ye Jehovah), and we should render personal hallelujahs to God daily in this church age, but only the ultimate future triumph of Christ will call forth the unanimous hallelujah of the universe. The twenty-four elders who join this chorus in Revelation 19 represent the ministry of the Word committed to the church, while the four living creatures represent all the agencies by which God's providential power works on earth. These "special interest" groups join all creation in the ultimate Hallelujah Chorus.

The Marriage Supper (19:9, 10)

The marriage supper, announced here in the fourth benediction of the Revelation,[1] seems to be distinct from the marriage of the Lamb. Verse 7 says literally, "The marriage of the Lamb *came*" (*ēlthen,* aorist tense). This past tense implies that the marriage actually took place at the rapture of Chapters 4 and 12. This distinguishes the bride of Christ from those that are "bidden" or called to the marriage supper of the Lamb (19:9). Note that John the Baptist said, "He that hath the bride is the bridegroom, but the *friend of the bridegroom,* that standeth and heareth him, rejoiceth greatly because of the bridegroom's voice" (John 3:29).

Psalm 45, which pictures the heavenly Bridegroom and his elect spouse, presents the king's daughter in the inner part of the palace (45:13), but there are also "virgins, her companions, that follow her." Part of the same picture is given by Jesus in his parable of the ten virgins in Matthew 25. The virgins should be kept distinct from the bride herself.

All of this imagery follows the ancient customs of marriage and its celebrations. First a betrothal was ratified in public between the two families involved, and this constituted the young couple legally man and wife. Then an interval followed during which the bridegroom and his father made preparations for the bride. When the father saw fit he would

---

[1]/Rev. 19:9; cf. 1:3; 14:13; 16:15.

send his son to the bride's home, and as the groom led the festive procession the cry would go out, "Behold, the bridegroom cometh!" Upon arriving at the home of the bride, the groom found that she too had made herself ready to be taken back to his home for a week or more of festivities. Here in Revelation, these festivities begin in 19:9, where the guests are bidden to the marriage supper of the Lamb. Some expositors feel that this is pressing the figures too far, but the parallels are too obvious to be overlooked.[2]

Although the benediction of 19:9 is not uttered by the Lord himself, it is part of his eleventh command to write.[3] The speaker of verse 9 is probably the same as in verse 5, where "a voice came forth from the throne." At first John thought the speaker was the Lord himself, but when he fell down at his feet to worship him, the speaker said, "See thou do it not; I am a fellow-servant with thee and with thy brethren that hold the testimony of Jesus; worship God, for the testimony of Jesus is the spirit of prophecy" (19:10). So this speaker is probably one of the saints of the Lamb and a fellow-servant with John.

The King of Kings (19:11-16)

In Revelation 15 only the sanctuary of heaven was opened for the seven bowl judgments, but in Revelation 19 the whole heaven opens for the exit of the King of kings and his armies. Some Bible expositors have mistakenly identified the white horse rider in Revelation 6 as Christ, and so will the Jews and the earth-dwellers of the Great Tribulation. But when Antichrist breaks his covenant with the Jews in the middle of the Tribulation, their eyes will be opened. Chapter 6 was too early for the revelation of the true Christ, but here in 19:11-16 Christ rides forth triumphantly on a white horse as the Faithful and True, "and in righteousness he doth judge and make war." Here is the battle which terminates the Great Tribulation and ends all wars for at least a thousand years.

Heaven itself opens dramatically for this majestic Rider

2/Cf. Matt. 25:1-10; Luke 19:35-40; 22:16.
3/See page 42.

with eyes as a flame of fire. On his head are many diadems, and on his garment are the bloodstains of his own sacrificial death. Accompanying him are all the white-robed armies of heaven mounted on white steeds.[4] Then a sharp sword proceeds out of the mouth of the Word of God incarnate, and he smites the nations and rules them with a rod of iron.[5] As a last act in cleansing the earth for his full repossession, Christ treads the winepress[6] of the fierceness of the wrath of God the Almighty by destroying the last wicked person on earth. Though he bears a name known only to himself, he also carries another title on his thigh—King of Kings and Lord of Lords. This is truly the Revelation of Jesus Christ!

The battle turns out to be a complete pushover for Christ, and the campaign mentioned in Chapters 14 and 16 is finally culminated. It is the last battle in the "war of the great day of God the Almighty" (16:14).

The Doom of the Beasts (19:17-21)

When Christ rides forth with the armies of heaven to take possession of the earth, the two wild Beasts together with the kings of the earth and their armies come to wage war against Christ and his hosts. However, the Lord of heaven overcomes all these enemies with lightning swiftness. The slaughter is so sudden and so complete that no one will be left to bury the dead! Instead, John sees an angel standing in the sun and summoning the birds of heaven to "Come and be gathered together unto the great supper of God, that ye may eat the flesh of kings, and the flesh of captains, and the flesh of mighty men, and the flesh of horses and of them that sit thereon, and the flesh of all men, both free and bond, and small and great" (19:17, 18). In Matthew Christ had said, "For as the lightning cometh forth from the east and is seen even unto the west, so shall be the coming of the Son of man. Wheresoever the carcass is, there will the eagles be gathered

---

4/Matt. 13:41; 24:31; Mark 8:38; 1 Cor. 6:2; Jude 14.
5/Psalm 2:9.
6/Isa. 63:1-3.

together."[7] Here we see the complete fulfillment of this prophecy, including the supper of the birds. They chose to "walk in the flesh," so now their flesh is eaten by birds!

Then follows the swift doom of the Beast and the false prophet. They are cast "alive into the lake of fire that burneth with brimstone" (19:20). The emphasis in this sentence is on the word "alive" (*zōntes,* living), for it comes first in the Greek sentence. This is significant because it means that the lake of fire is a real place[8] and that its agonies are just as real and infinitely more intense than any sufferings that we can experience now on earth. The consignment of the wicked to the lake of fire fulfills Paul's prophecy in 2 Thessalonians 2:8—"And then shall be revealed the lawless one, whom the Lord Jesus shall slay with the breath of his mouth, and bring to nought by the manifestation of his coming." Thus ends the earthly existence of the Antichrist and the false prophet. They are far from being annihilated, however, for their sufferings will be as endless as God himself (20:10).

THE REIGN OF CHRIST (20:1-15)

The purpose of the *revelation* of Christ is to prepare for the reign of Christ. The Millennium can be thought of as God's final trial of sinful man before the eternal ages. The trial began in the Garden of Eden with the Age of Innocence, and it has continued through the successive ages of Conscience, Human Government, Promise, Law, and Grace. Soon we will be at the threshold of the Millennium. The common denominator of all these ages is the deceptive and wicked heart of man, shown either in secret rebellion or in open defiance of the righteous rule of the sovereign God. Even during

---

7/Matt. 24:27, 28; cf. Deut. 28:26; Jer. 7:33; 16:4; Ezek. 29:17-20.
8/The lake of fire in 20:10, 14, 15; 21:8 is the same as Gehenna in Matt. 5:22, 29, 30; 10:28; 18:9; 23:15, 33; Mark 9:43, 45, 47; Luke 12:5; James 3:6. Cf. Matt. 25:41 with Rev. 20:10. Gehenna is not to be confused with Sheol of the Old Testament or with hades of the New Testament. Sheol and hades are both the same place—the place of departed spirits described by Christ in Luke 16:19-31. Neither one is the final abode of the wicked, but finally death and hades are to be cast into the lake of fire (Rev. 20:14).

the nearly ideal Millennium man's secret rebellion against God will ultimately explode into open defiance against the Almighty.

The Binding of Satan (20:1-3)

The doom of the Beast and the false prophet was only part of God's judgment, for the war of the great day of God the Almighty does not end until Satan himself is chained and cast into the abyss. In 20:2 he is described by the same four names as in Revelation 12:9—Dragon, Old Serpent, Devil, and Satan. These have their counterpart in the four names of the white horse rider of Chapter 19: Faithful, True, King of kings, and Lord of lords.

The name *Dragon* reminds us of all the earthly political powers which Satan gave to the first Beast, the Antichrist. *Old Serpent* recalls his subtle existence from the very beginning of human history and down through the ages of time. *Devil* calls to mind Satan's slanderous, murderous, blasphemous, and lying character.[9] *Satan* shows him to be the adversary and accuser who disputes Christ's right to reign. Who could challenge such a being except Christ himself? The most likely interpretation of the "angel" in 20:1 is therefore the same as that of 10:1-7 and 18:1, 21, namely, the Angel of Jehovah, Christ himself. Though Michael the archangel was commissioned to wage war against Satan in Chapter 12, here in Chapter 20 the Devil is personally chained and cast into the abyss for a thousand years. Only Christ is capable of doing this. In Revelation 1:18 he holds the keys of death and hades, and here in Chapter 20 he carries the key of the abyss. In other words, Christ's appearances in Revelation vary according to the work to be done. Since Satan himself is an angel, the Personage who chains him is represented as the Angel of Jehovah.

What kind of chain is this? The Bible does not specify iron, brass, or any other tangible material. The chain is instead a spirit-chain, just as the horses of heaven are spirit-horses. Yet this chain is so durable that it can bind spirits and

---

[9]/John 8:44.

fetter angels. Jude tells of such chains which now hold fallen angels (Jude 6). The chain here in Revelation 20 is therefore a literal spirit-chain. Seiss says, "Figures, tropes, and shadows cannot bind anybody, unless it be some commentators, who seem to be hopelessly entangled by them."[10] So Satan is chained in the same abyss from which the Beast (17:8) and spirit-locusts came (9:1-3).

Some commentators believe that the binding of Satan took place at the beginning of the church age, but if so, Peter was mistaken when he said, "Your adversary, the devil, as a roaring lion walketh about, seeking whom he may devour" (1 Pet. 5:8). To believe that Satan is bound in this age is to close our eyes to the diabolical persecutions of all the Neros, Hitlers, and Stalins of the last two thousand years. No, Christ's thousand-year reign begins not with the Cross or Pentecost, but just as the Revelation predicts it—at the personal return of Christ in glory (19:11-16). The binding of Satan is just one of the preparations for this glorious reign of peace.

The First Resurrection (20:4-6)

Like the rapture, the first resurrection occurs in phases over a period of time, beginning with the resurrection of Christ, the firstfruits.[11] Shortly after Christ's resurrection many bodies of the saints that had been exposed by the earthquake in Jerusalem arose alive out of their graves.[12] This demonstration in the very first century of the church age is a precursor to the phases of the first resurrection that will occur before and during the Great Tribulation. The phases of the resurrection coincide with those of the rapture, for translation presupposes resurrection. The resurrected saints include the elders and living creatures of Revelation 4, the great multitude of Gentiles in Chapter 7, the two witnesses of Chapter 11, the man-child of Chapter 12, the 144,000 Israelites of Chapter 14, and the harvest of saints in Chapter 14.

10/Seiss, *op. cit.,* Lecture 44.
11/1 Cor. 15:23, 24.
12/Matt. 27:52, 53.

The word "resurrection" is used in the New Testament only to denote the arising of a physical body from the grave. The *first* resurrection here in Revelation 20:6 presupposes a *second* resurrection, that of the wicked dead after the Millennium. The first resurrection includes saints only, and it occurs before and during the Great Tribulation. If words mean anything, Revelation 20 teaches *two* resurrections rather than a single general resurrection at the end of the Millennium.

Why does the first resurrection occur before the Millennium? So that Christ's saints may reign with him as a kingdom of priests unto God the Father.[13] This plan was promised to the overcomer in Christ's message to Thyatira: "He that overcometh, and he that keepeth my works unto the end, to him will I give authority over the nations; and he shall rule them with a rod of iron" (2:26, 27).[14]

The word "souls" (*psuchás*) is a synecdoche for "persons." It denotes embodied individuals, as in Acts 2:41 and 27:37. These "souls" have been previously resurrected and translated. Colossians 3:4 says, "When Christ, who is our life, shall be manifested, then shall ye also with him be manifested in glory."

In the second resurrection everyone will be resurrected at the same time, with the exception of the Beast and the false prophet, who are already in the lake of fire. But the saints will have been rewarded a millennium earlier.

Think of the tremendous revolution that will follow the first resurrection! Dominion will be transferred from the "almighty dollar" to the Almighty Christ. All the haunts of sin and debauchery, all the affiliations of crime and commerce, and all the unholy combinations of religion and fornication will suddenly be transformed to temples of worship, relationships of righteousness, and activities of holiness. All this and infinitely more will flow from the reigning Christ, for he and his saints will shepherd the nations with a rod of iron. The saints will be kept busy, for the Millennium will be an age of

---

13/Rev. 1:6.
14/See also 1 Pet. 2:9; 5:4; Dan. 7:26, 27; 2 Tim. 2:3-5; 4:7, 8; Luke 12:32; Rev. 3:11; Matt. 19:28; 1 Cor. 6:2.

activity and work—not just a thousand years of idleness. But the work will be a joy, for righteousness and peace will reign, and men will truly love one another. Part of the work will include the duties of royal priesthood (1:6; 5:10), for the fifth benediction of Revelation (20:6) tells us that we will reign a thousand years as priests of God and of Christ. The long-promised millennial rest is therefore not idleness but a welcome reprieve from the curse of sin and the strife of selfishness. Heaven is a place of ceaseless praise and unending activity. Hallelujah, for the Lord God omnipotent reigneth!

That the Millennium is not ushered in gradually is proved by the crime and consternation of our present age of war and strife. Only Christ can introduce the Millennium, and he will do this only when he personally returns to reign. Notice the following comparisons between the church age and the millennial age.

The Church Age	*The Millennial Age*
1. The saints are pilgrims and strangers (Heb. 11:13).	1. The saints are a kingdom—priests unto God (1:6).
2. The saints are to expect persecution (Matt. 5:11; 1 Cor. 4:12; 2 Tim. 3:12).	2. The saints will be promoted to places of royal priesthood (1 Pet. 5:4).
3. The church is commissioned to teach all nations (Matt. 28:19, 20).	3. Under the new covenant with Israel there will be little need for teaching, for all will know Jehovah (Jer. 31:34).
4. The church now observes the ordinances of baptism and the Lord's Supper (1 Cor. 11:26), but only "till he come."	4. The Jews in the Millennium will offer animal sacrifices as a *memorial* of the Cross (Ezek. 43:18-27; 44:11-31; 45:13—46:15).
5. Israel is now in unbelief (Rom. 11:20-32).	5. Israel will be saved as a nation (Rom. 11:26).

6. God is longsuffering in this age of grace (2 Pet. 3:9).

6. God will rule rigorously in the Millennium (Isa. 2:4; 9:7).

7. Now there are wars and rumors of wars (Matt. 24:6).

7. Then there will be 1000 years of peace (Isa. 2:4; Joel 3:10; Mic. 4:3).

8. Now the curse binds all creation, including mankind (Rom. 8:22).

8. Then the curse will be lifted from all creation, including mankind (Rom. 8:23, 24).

9. Now Satan goes about as a roaring lion, seeking whom he may devour (1 Pet. 5:8).

9. Then Satan will be bound with a spirit-chain in the abyss (Rev. 20:10; cf. 21:1-4).

10. Now Satan is the god of this age and a usurper of the authority of Christ (2 Cor. 4:4).

10. Then Christ will reign as King of kings and Lord of lords (Rev. 20:6).

11. Now wickedness is rampant (2 Tim. 3).

11. Then wickedness will be restrained (Isa. 2:12-22; 11:9; Heb. 2:14).

12. Now sickness and death hold sway.

12. Then "the inhabitant shall not say, I am sick" (Isa. 33:24), and death will be rare (Isa. 65:20-23).

13. Now ferocious beasts are the enemies of mankind, and man is the destructive enemy of the animal kingdom.

13. Then the child will play on the hole of the asp, and the wolf will dwell safely with the lamb (Isa. 11:6-9).

The Loosing of Satan (20:7-10)

Despite all the many blessings of the Millennium, it is not a totally perfect age. The Millennium is not the eternal state of Revelation 21 and 22, though it is surely a great step toward perfection. The end of the Millennium does not mark the end of the reign of Christ and his saints, nor does it spell the end of human habitation on earth. Christ's kingdom will be an everlasting kingdom, and the people who live on the new and eternal earth will fulfill God's original purpose in creating Adam, for no purpose of God is ever eternally thwarted. The millennial age is therefore the final test of mankind just before the eternal ages begin. This test is completed by releasing Satan for a short time. The newly-emancipated deceiver then seduces Gog and Magog into an unsuccessful, last-ditch rebellion against Christ and his saints.

This release of Satan (20:7) shows that the thousand years of imprisonment produced no reform in his character; nor did the thousand years of Christ's righteous reign change the wicked hearts of multitudes of people born during the Millennium. The same old Serpent that deceived Eve now seduces a great multitude of people called "Gog and Magog." Whether this group is identical with the Gog and Magog of Ezekiel 38 or is merely a symbolic name is debatable. In any case, Satan successfully attracts those people who have been only outwardly loyal to the rule of Christ and his saints. Then he deceives them into believing they can successfully overthrow Christ's whole divine monarchy. So Satan's swarming multitudes group around the camp of God's saints and the beloved city (20:9). But before Satan actually begins his attack, the fire of God falls from heaven and devours the wicked. This ends God's purpose for Satan, and he is now "cast into the lake of fire and brimstone, where are also the beast and the false prophet; and they shall be tormented day and night forever and ever" (20:10).[15] So the final doom of the nations and the final doom of Satan occur at the same time. There is no description of the battle, for it is simply another pushover for Christ!

The Great White Throne (20:11-15)

All that remains to complete the Millennium is the great white throne judgment, which includes the second resurrection and the doom of unbelievers. This throne may be identified with the scene in Revelation 4 and 5, for when the enthroned

---

15/Cf. Matt. 25:46.

One appears in all his tremendous majesty and mystery, the glory of his countenance causes heaven and earth to flee away. Here we see the indescribable, mysterious, and eternal Godhead, including the enthroned Father, the eternal Son, and the sevenfold Holy Spirit.

The flight of heaven and earth is a highly poetic way of describing the re-genesis of all things and the awesomeness of God's majestic presence. A graphic description of the re-generated heavens and earth follows in Revelation 21 and 22.

At the time of the great white throne judgment all sinners are resurrected to stand before God. No trumpet signals the event (as in the first resurrection), for this awesome second resurrection is effected by the quiet power of the Holy Trinity. All unsaved sinners—great and small, rich and poor—stand exposed before the throne of the Almighty. There are no white robes, no crowns, and no palms—only naked sinners whose works condemn them to share the lake of fire forever with the trinity of evil. Each sinner is judged according to his own works (20:12). God has kept accurate records; all the books are there. Even the Book of Life is there, lest any condemned person claims a right to heaven. The awful blots where their names might have been will testify silently, "I never knew you" (Matt. 7:23). In these books every evil deed and every evil thought of every sinner will be indelibly recorded and justly punished. The book of memory will be there too, to remind the condemned of long-forgotten sins. And the book of conscience will be there, convicting men of sins which their hardened consciences had glossed over. The book of words and deeds will serve as an accurate basis for judgment. And the books of the Bible will remind the unbelievers of the good news which they spurned. The book of God's revelation in nature will be used as a basis for judging those who did not have access to God's Word. They will all be without excuse.[16]

Regardless of the degree of punishment, the destiny of all who experience the second resurrection is "the lake of fire and brimstone." What else could God say to mortal man to de-

---

[16]/Rom. 1:20.

scribe this horrible place? If the fire is not physical, it is nevertheless real. It is a fire which torments both body and spirit. God calls this eternal torment the second death—not annihilation. "They shall be tormented," he says, "day and night forever and ever" (20:10).

Death and hades are also cast into the lake of fire. The use of the definite article before each of these two words shows that they represent two distinct concepts. The casting of "death" into the lake of fire means that death is forever banished from the universe; no one will ever die again.[17] The casting of hades into the lake of fire means that the temporal place of departed spirits is emptied out and is also gone forever. Everything that remains becomes a part of eternity. Death, hades,[18] the Beast, the false prophet, and Satan are all in the lake of fire with their victims, the countless millions of wicked dead. But the millennial saints go to the new earth, described in Revelation 21 and 22.

SUMMARY

The day of the Lord began in Revelation 6 and continued throughout the Great Tribulation and the entire millennial age. This "day" is briefly summarized by Peter in these words:

> But the day of the Lord will come as a thief in the night, in the which the heavens shall pass away with a great noise and the elements shall be dissolved with fervent heat, and the earth and the works that are therein shall be burned up. Seeing that these things are thus all to be dissolved, what manner of persons ought ye to be in all holy living and godliness, looking for and earnestly desiring the coming of the day of God, by reason of which the heavens being on fire shall be dissolved, and the elements shall melt with fervent

---

[17]/1 Cor. 15:26, 54, 55; cf. Rom. 5:12.
[18]/Hades (*hádēs*) is found in Rev. 1:18; 6:8; 20:13, 14; and each time it is associated with *death*.

heat? But according to his promise, we look for new heavens and a new earth, wherein dwelleth righteousness.[19]

This Scripture serves as a fitting close to Revelation 20 and an enlightening introduction to Chapter 21.

In Revelation 19 and 20 we saw Christ's public revelation as King of kings and Lord of lords, the doom of the Antichrist and the false prophet, the binding of Satan and the thousand-year reign of Christ with his resurrected saints, the temporary release of Satan and his subsequent deception of the nations, the final doom of Satan and the nations, and the great white throne judgment with its resurrection and condemnation of all unsaved people. This brings us to the very threshold of the eternal ages, described in the last two chapters of Revelation.

[19]/2 Pet. 3:10-13.

PART FIVE

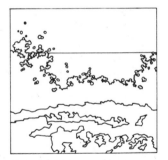

CHRIST
IN THE CONSUMMATION

15

CHRIST CREATES IN THE CONSUMMATION

Revelation 21, 22

INSTRUCTIONS FOR STUDYING REVELATION 21 AND 22

Read Genesis 2 as your devotional approach to these wonderful chapters in Revelation. Thank God for what he has prepared for you in eternity. Paradise lost is now paradise regained! Use all the study methods you have learned as you research Revelation 21 and 22. Finish all your charts and projects.

1. Read 2 Peter 3:10-13 and relate the passage chronologically to Revelation.
2. List the "new" things recorded in Revelation 21 and 22 and make significant observations about them.
3. What is the significance of the word "new"? Does it mean that the first heaven and first earth are annihilated by the great burning, or does it simply mean that they are purged? What does "passing away" mean in 21:4? Compare these Scriptures with Isaiah 65:17; 66:22. The Greek word for "new" in Revelation 2:17; 3:12; 5:9; 14:3; 21:1, 2, 5 is *kainós* (meaning *new in quality*) and *néos* (meaning *new in time*). For a full discussion of these

synonyms see Trench, *op. cit.,* pages 219-225.
4. What is the significance of John's double vision of the Holy City's descent (21:2 and 21:10)?
5. Compare God's last promise to the overcomer (21:7) with Christ's seven promises to the overcomer in Revelation 2 and 3.
6. How does Chapter 21 relate the judgment of the bowls to the blessing of the "new things"?
7. Why is the Holy City called "the bride, the wife of the Lamb" in 21:9? Is this a literal place? Compare John 14:1-6.
8. Will the saints' reign with Christ end at the close of the millennial age? Explain.
9. List the references to the imminence of Christ's coming in the epilogue (22:6-21). What is the significance of each reference?
10. Complete your list of "blesseds" in Revelation and indicate the significance of the two in the epilogue.
11. How does the epilogue attest the genuineness and authenticity of the Revelation?

NOTES ON REVELATION 21, 22

CHRIST RENEWING (21:1—22:5)

The first great showing in the Revelation of Jesus Christ began in 1:9 and was seen from the Isle of Patmos. It included the vision of Christ in Chapter 1 and his central position in the churches in Chapters 2 and 3. The second great showing began in heaven and spanned Chapters 4 through 16. This vision included the throne in heaven, the seven-sealed book, the seven trumpet judgments, the seven personages, and the seven bowl judgments, all displaying Christ in the conflict. The third great showing began in the wilderness and covered Chapters 17 through 20. It included the seven dooms, the revelation of Jesus Christ from heaven, and the millennial reign of Christ on earth, all revealing Christ in the conquest. The fourth great showing of Revelation begins in Chapter 21 and continues through the fifth verse of Chapter 22. This last showing includes the seven new things of the eternal ages, and it presents Christ in the consummation as he makes all things new. Then follows the epilogue, which shows Christ inviting all who are thirsty to partake freely of the water of life.

The Bride of the Lamb (21:1-8)

The bride of the Lamb is seen by John from two different viewpoints—first as the *bride* of the Lamb and then as the *wife* of the Lamb. In each case she is identified with the Holy City, New Jerusalem, her dwellingplace. This reminds us that mere edifices and avenues do not make a city, even as mortar and bricks do not make a home. A true city or home requires living personalities. When hundreds of students leave a college campus for vacation, the few remaining personnel often exclaim, "This place is like a morgue!" This means, of course, that the school is made up of living personalities even more than mere buildings and equipment. The New Jerusalem of the eternal ages is a real place, but it cannot be thought of apart from its inhabitants.

In his first vision of the Holy City John sees a comprehensive picture of all things made new (21:5). The four new things specifically mentioned include a new heaven, a new earth, new peoples and the New Jerusalem. The new heaven and new earth replace the former heaven and earth that "fled away" from the face of the enthroned Father (20: 11). In his eschatological discourse to his disciples, Jesus said, "Heaven and earth shall pass away, but my words shall not pass away."[1] Isaiah said, "For, behold, I create new heavens and a new earth; and the former things shall not be remembered, nor come into mind. . . . For as the new heavens and the new earth, which I will make, shall remain before me, saith Jehovah, so shall your seed and your name remain" (65:17; 66:22). Peter said,

> Seeing that these things are thus all to be dissolved,
> what manner of persons ought ye to be in all holy

---

[1]/Matt. 24:35; Mark 13:31; Luke 21:33.

living and godliness, looking for and earnestly desiring the coming of the day of God, by reason of which the heavens being on fire shall be dissolved, and the elements shall melt with fervent heat? But, according to his promise, we look for new heavens and a new earth, wherein dwelleth righteousness.[2]

Chronologically, this section from 2 Peter would fit between Revelation 20 and 21. Some expositors feel that these Scriptures indicate nothing more than a renovation of the physical heavens and earth by the purifying fires of God's righteous judgments. Others feel that the use of the words "create," "fled away," "there was found no place for them," and "new" (*kainós*) indicate that a creative act of God is involved. Since *kainós* connotes pristine quality as opposed to wear and deterioration from long use, Revelation 21:1, 5 seems to imply that God will create an entirely new heaven and earth. Whichever view is correct, the heavenlies which are now misused and defiled by evil spirit beings will pass away to make room for the new heaven. Moreover, the earth which now groans under the curse of sin and disease will give way to the new earth, in which righteousness reigns. The earthly Jerusalem, which has been destroyed so many times because of sin and unbelief, will be replaced by the Holy City, the New Jerusalem, and will look like a bride adorned for her husband (21:2). And the present fallen race of mankind will be replaced by saints redeemed and renewed through the cleansing blood of the slain Lamb, for "if any man is in Christ, he is a new creature; the old things are passed away; behold, they are become new" (2 Cor. 5:17).

This miraculous change in the heart of man makes it possible for the tabernacle of God to be with men, so that he can dwell with them as he did with Adam before the fall (21:3). The old separation occasioned by the fall of man in Genesis 3 has at last been cancelled. God's heaven, the new physical heavens, and the new earth have been joined together in the fellowship which God intended in his original creation. This truth is emphasized by the three "with" phrases in Revelation

---

[2]/2 Pet. 3:11-13.

21:3—"The tabernacle of God is *with* men, and he shall dwell *with* them, and they shall be his peoples, and God himself shall be *with* them, and be their God." The result of this great reconciliation of God and man through the Cross of Christ is eternal union and communion with God. A few of the blessings which result from such union and communion are shown in verse 4: "And he shall wipe away every tear from their eyes; and death shall be no more; neither shall there be mourning, nor crying, nor pain any more." Instead, the water of life will be granted freely, and the overcomer will inherit all these new things. More important still, "I will be his God, and he shall be my son" (21:7). This is the eighth promise to the overcomer, and since eight is the number of Christ, he becomes all in all.

A list of the people excluded from this eternal bliss follows the last promise to the overcomer, serving as a warning to any presumptuous reader who may be trusting in some past experience rather than in a present relationship with Christ. "But for the fearful, and unbelieving, and abominable, and murderers, and fornicators, and sorcerers, and idolaters, and all liars, their part shall be in the lake that burneth with fire and brimstone, which is the second death" (21:8). Everyone who falls under any of these descriptions will be excluded from the bride of the Lamb and will be banished from the presence of God forever.

The Wife of the Lamb (21:9—22:5)

After John saw all things made new, he was carried away "in the Spirit to a mountain great and high" to see "the bride, the wife of the Lamb" coming down out of heaven from God. From this second vantage point John saw further details about the Holy City. This time the bride is seen as the wife of the Lamb, for the consummated marriage has produced an eternal relationship of intimate spiritual union.

The city is resplendent with the glory of God, and her light is like that of a rare scintillating jasper. The whole sight contrasts dramatically with John's wilderness vision of the judgment of the great whore (17:1). There John saw the culmination of all that was wicked and abominable, but here he sees the wife of the Lamb glowing radiantly in Christ's glory.

The fact that it was "one of the seven angels who had the seven bowls" (21:9) who invited John to this mountain vantage point suggests that it was necessary to finish the Great Tribulation judgments before God could bestow his universal and eternal blessings (16:7; 21:6, 9). Now there will be no further need for judgment, for sin will have been banished forever from the universe.

The Holy City offers ample room for all the saints, for it measures twelve thousand furlongs (about fifteen hundred miles) in each direction. This is about the distance from northern Maine to southern Florida! Since the city is a perfect cube, it reminds us of the Old Testament holy of holies in both the tabernacle and the temple. The four high walls of the city are inlaid with jasper stones, and each of the twelve gates (three to a wall) is made of a single pearl. The gates are adorned by twelve sentinel angels and are inscribed with the names of the twelve tribes of Israel. The twelve foundations are engraved with the names of the twelve apostles of the Lamb and are made of twelve different kinds of precious stones (21:19, 20). The engravings of these twenty-four names on the gates and foundations helps confirm the identity of the twenty-four elders mentioned in Chapter 4.[3]

The city is "pure gold, like unto pure glass" (21:18), and its main street is also paved with gold (21:21). The unique nature of this gold and the difficulty of identifying the precious stones of the city with present-day jewels tells us that the New Jerusalem is beautiful beyond human description or imagination. The name of each apostle on a different kind of precious stone suggests the different personalities through which the gospel message is conveyed. Each apostle had his own individual gift, and God used each in his own unique way. Just as it took all twelve apostles to lay the foundation in their day,[4] so Christ is looking to each member of his body to accomplish a particular purpose in this present age.

---

[3]/See page 68.
[4]/Eph. 2:20.

In addition to the four new things which John saw from the viewpoint of verses 2 through 8, the latter part of Chapter 21 calls attention to three more: the new temple, the new light, and the new life. The new temple (21:22) is really not a building at all, for the Lord God Almighty and the Lamb himself are the true center of worship. On the old earth there was a sanctuary in the tabernacle and temple in which the invisible God met his worshipers, but the veil constantly hid the manifestation of God's glory. In New Testament times little importance was attached to earthly temples, for Christ had taught that worship was to be "in Spirit and in truth." But in the eternal ages man is in the actual presence of God the Almighty and the Lamb (21:22). He therefore needs no temple to remind him of God's presence, for he is in the eternal presence of the omnipresent God.

The new light is the glory of God, so there is no need of sun, moon, or stars. The nations and kings of the earth now enjoy the full radiance of God's presence—a radiance that would utterly consume man in his sinful condition today. A single small ray of this glory blinded Saul as the persecutor traveled to Damascus. No wonder verse 27 says, "There shall in no wise enter into it anything unclean, or he that maketh an abomination and a lie, but only they that are written in the Lamb's book of life" (21:27)! The full glory of God's presence would instantly consume every sinner.

The new life (22:1-5) is the seventh new thing of Chapters 21 and 22. This new life is symbolized by the "river of water, bright as crystal, proceeding out of the throne of God and of the Lamb." It is also symbolized by "the tree of life, bearing twelve manner of fruits, yielding its fruit every month; and the leaves of the tree were for the healing of the nations." The tree of life that was removed from man after his fall has now been restored.[5] Paradise lost is now paradise regained.[6] And the eternal paradise will be a place of service as well as

---

[5]/Cf. Gen. 2:9; 3:24.

[6]/The word used for tree here is *zúlon* (wood) rather than *déndron* (tree). This word is also used for the "cross" of Christ in Acts 5:30; 10:39; 13:29; Gal. 3:13; 1 Pet. 2:24. This should remind the reader that the regaining of paradise cost the Lamb his very life's blood.

of reigning. "His slaves shall serve him; and they shall see his face; and his name shall be on their foreheads . . . and they shall reign forever and ever" (22:3-5; cf. 1:6). So the overcomers will reign with Christ not only during the millennial age but all through the ages of eternity.

CHRIST CALLING (22:6-21)

Since the four great showings of the Revelation of Jesus Christ end at 22:5, John must receive the epilogue (22:6-21) by some other method. Even as God used an angel to form a connection between John's senses and the future events which the angel was to "televise" (1:1, 2), so here God employs an angel to convey the utterances of "the Lord, the God of the spirits of the prophets" (22:6). So the words conveyed are those of the Father and the Son. The epilogue closes both the Revelation and the entire canon of Scripture. It serves as a divine seal to the inspiration, authority, and absolute verbal accuracy of this book in particular and the Bible in general. In these closing words Christ calls the thirsty reader to come to the living fountain and take freely of the water of life.

The Testimony of the Father (22:6-15)

The four visions which John saw were not simply mental pictures from his imagination but objective previews of actual future events. These John faithfully recorded as he saw the events unfold. Two unimpeachable witnesses—God the Father and God the Son—testify to the truthfulness of the words which John penned.[7]

The first endorsement comes from the Father, and it contains four announcements of the imminence of Christ's coming. The first emphasis on imminence occurs in 22:6, and it declares that these things "must shortly (*en táchei*) come to pass." *En táchei* occurs twice in Revelation—here and in 1:1. It means "quickly, at once, without delay, soon, in a short

---

[7]/Rev. 19:9; 21:5; 22:6, 16. Cf. Deut. 17:6; 19:15; John 5:31-37; 8:17; 2 Cor. 13:1; Heb. 10:28; Rev. 11:3, which indicate the necessity of two witnesses.

time." The emphasis in 22:6 is on *attestation* of Christ's imminence.

The second emphasis on imminence is in verse 7—"I come quickly" (*érchomai tachú*). *Tachú* occurs six times in Revelation,[8] and four of these refer to the actions of Christ. It means "without delay, quickly, at once." Christians should be more concerned about the actions of Christ and his personal return than they are about identifying the Antichrist. The Scriptures nowhere tell us to look for the Antichrist, but we are constantly reminded to look for our blessed Lord. Since this announcement is followed by the sixth "blessed," and since the blessing is promised to the one "that keepeth the words of the prophecy of this book," the emphasis is on *obedience*. John's immediate reaction to these wonderful words is an impulse to worship the one who transmitted them, mistaking the servile angel for Christ himself (22:8). This is the second time that John mistook an angel for Christ (cf. 19:10), but once again the angel said to him, "See thou do it not: I am a fellow-servant with thee and with thy brethren the prophets, and with them that keep the words of this book: worship God" (22:9). The very fact that John was mistaken on both these occasions confirms the inspiration of the words that were spoken. He sensed that such words could come only from his blessed Lord.

The third emphasis on the imminence of the fulfillment of these prophecies is in verse 10—"Seal not up the words of the prophecy of this book, for the time is at hand." Since the next verse contains both a warning and an admonition, the emphasis is on *preparation*. The command to "seal not"[9] is a litotes, expressing negatively what is intended positively, namely, to proclaim the words of the prophecy of this book. Not everyone will believe them; in many cases the unrighteous will become still more ungodly and the filthy even more debauched. But, thank God, in even more cases the proclamation of these blessed words will cause the righteous to become more godly and the holy to become more Christlike. The

---

8/Rev. 2:16; 3:11; 11:14; 22:7, 12, 20. Many cursives and printed texts include *tachú* in 2:5.
9/Cf. Dan. 12:4, 9.

responsibility of the proclaimer, then, is to preach the Word, and the responsibility of God is to produce results. If the preaching of the truths of Revelation does not effect a change in the lives of those who hear, there is no other way to bring men to repentance. The same can be said about all the other books of the Bible. There will come a time when it is impossible to change one's spiritual condition. The eternal state will be fixed forever, either in heaven with the redeemed or in the lake of fire with the damned.

The fourth emphasis on the imminence of Christ's return occurs in verse 12—"Behold, I come quickly; and my reward is with me, to render to each man according as his work is." The emphasis here is on *reward,* and this emphasis is also seen in the seventh "blessed" which follows: "Blessed are they that wash their robes, that they may have the right to come to the tree of life, and may enter in by the gates into the city" (22:14).[10] Beginning at 1:7, "behold" (*idou*) is used thirty times in the Revelation, and at least seven of these call attention to the Lord's coming. The washing of the saints' robes results from the purifying hope of the Lord's return, for personal purification is one of the most important implications of the blessed hope. This is John's emphasis in his First Epistle:

> Beloved, now are we children of God, and it is not yet made manifest what we shall be. We know that if he shall be manifested we shall be like him, for we shall see him even as he is. And everyone that hath this hope set on him purifieth himself, even as he is pure.[11]

The coming of the Lord and the readiness of the Christian are always related to reward. Second Timothy 4:8 says, "Henceforth there is laid up for me the crown of righteousness, which the Lord, the righteous judge, shall give to me at that day; and not to me only, but also to all them that have loved his appearing." Titus 2:13 exhorts us to be "looking for the blessed hope and appearing of the glory of the great God

---

10/Cf. Rev. 1:3; 14:13; 16:15; 19:9; 20:6; 22:7, 14.
11/1 John 3:2, 3.

and our Saviour Jesus Christ." Hebrews 9:28 presents the Christ who "shall appear a second time apart from sin to them that wait for him, unto salvation." Revelation 16:15 describes the coming of Christ "as a thief"—that is, unannounced. Then follows "Blessed is he that watcheth and keepeth his garments, lest he walk naked and they see his shame." Those servants who neglected to wash their robes were therefore not privileged to escape the Great Tribulation.[12] They said, "My Lord delayeth his coming,"[13] and were left to suffer at least part of the Antichrist's persecutions.[14]

Those who "have the right to come to the tree of life" (22:14) during the eternal ages are those who have washed their robes, for nothing unclean will be allowed to enter the gates of the Holy City. "Without are the dogs,[15] and the sorcerers, and the fornicators, and the murderers, and the idolators, and everyone that loveth and maketh a lie" (22:15). These sins do not look any better in the lives of Christians than they do in the lives of sinners; in fact, they look worse. They are not the fruit of the Spirit but the works of the flesh. Galatians 5:21 says, "I forewarn you, even as I did forewarn you, that they who practise such things shall not inherit the kingdom of God."

The Testimony of the Son (22:16-21)

The testimony of the Son is now added to the testimony of the Father: "I Jesus have sent mine angel to testify unto you these things for the churches. I am the root and the offspring of David,[16] the bright, the morning star" (22:16; cf. 2:28). So the Revelation of Jesus Christ is designed especially for the church, so that Christ "might sanctify it, having cleansed it by the washing of water with the word, that he might present the church to himself a glorious church, not having

---

12/Cf. Rev. 4 and 12 with Rev. 7 and 14.
13/Luke 12:45; Matt. 24:48.
14/See Appendix 3 for Chronological Ribbon Chart.
15/Cf. Deut. 23:18; Matt. 7:6; 15:26; Rom. 1:26, 27.
16/Isa. 11:10.

spot or wrinkle or any such thing; but that it should be holy and without blemish."[17]

This endorsement of Christ contains the twofold invitation of the Spirit and the bride, who both say, "Come; and he that heareth, let him say, Come. And he that is athirst, let him come; he that will, let him take the water of life freely" (22:17). This leaves man without excuse. Even where there is no written revelation in certain remote corners of the earth, "The Spirit bloweth where he will,"[18] and "the invisible things of him since the creation of the world are clearly seen, being perceived through the things that are made, even his everlasting power and divinity, that they may be without excuse."[19]

Then follows the warning against adding to or taking from the words of the prophecy of this Book. For a person to add human words to these divine words would be to add to himself the plagues recorded in the Book. To take away from the sacred words which God authorized Christ to give us would be to take away our right to eat of the tree of life and to forfeit our privilege of living in the Holy City. While this warning applies specifically to the Revelation, it also applies to the whole Bible, for "All Scripture is given by inspiration of God, and is profitable for doctrine, for reproof, for correction, for instruction in righteousness, that the man of God may be perfect, throughly furnished unto all good works."[20]

This testimony of the Son also includes the fifth emphasis in the epilogue on the imminence of Christ's coming. "I come quickly" (22:20) is followed by "Amen; come, Lord Jesus," the last prayer of the Bible. In other words, our attitude toward this blessed hope should be not only that of obedience and resignation but also that of positive prayer for Christ's soon return. Only then can his will be done in the earth, as it is in heaven.

The New Testament has more references to Christ's second coming than it has pages. Christ's return was the main

[17]/Eph. 5:26, 27.
[18]/John 3:8, free translation.
[19]/Rom. 1:20.
[20]/2 Tim. 3:16, 17, KJV.

subject of the Old Testament prophecies, and it is the only hope for our present age.

After the last announcement of Christ's coming and the last prayer of the Bible, John adds his own benediction upon the reader: "The grace of the Lord Jesus be with the saints. Amen."

SUMMARY

Chapters 21 and 22 contain the last great showing of Revelation as well as the epilogue to the whole Book. Here Christ is seen making all things new in the consummation. The seven new things specifically mentioned include the new heavens, the new earth, the New Jerusalem, the new peoples, the new temple, the new light, and the new life. The New Jerusalem appears under the figure of the bride of the Lamb and the wife of the Lamb.

The epilogue in Chapter 22 provides the testimony of God the Father and God the Son, and this testimony serves as a divine seal to the inspiration of the whole book. Included in this twofold testimony are five references to the imminence of Christ's return and the fulfilment of the prophecies of this book. The emphasis in these announcements is on our personal attestation, obedience, preparation, reward, and prayer.

16

OUR APPROPRIATE RESPONSE
TO THE REVELATION

During this thrilling adventure of independent Bible study in the Revelation of Jesus Christ, we have seen many things which were beyond the power of human language to describe. Yet everything we have truly learned is ours to enjoy forever.

First we saw the consummation of God's plan of redemption—that great plan which began even before the foundation of the world. In spite of the failure and fall of man with its consequent guilt of soul and curse on creation, the Revelation unveils man's full restoration to eternal fellowship with God in the New Jerusalem. Even the earth itself is made new, and all its inhabitants will at last be sinless forever.

Exactly when these "last things" will begin the Revelation does not say. Men of every generation since A.D. 95 have tried to identify these prophecies with current events, and some have unwisely set specific dates for Christ's return. But one thing is certain: Jesus is coming back personally to reign. Many recent events have fulfilled long-awaited prophecies and point to the possibility that the "second showing" (4:1) of Revelation may begin at any time. Some of these recently-realized prophecies are the return of the Jew to Palestine in

1948, the apparent beginnings of a ten-kingdom confederacy in the Mediterranean area of the old Roman Empire under the name of the European Common Market, the international movement of Protestants and Roman Catholics toward a one-world church, the Jewish conquest of the whole city of Jerusalem on June 7, 1967, for the first time since A.D. 70, and the developing search for a unique political leader who can solve world problems. War-weary mankind will probably sell out to the first plausible candidate for world peace, and the tyranny of the Antichrist will follow in short order.

The Revelation, however, focuses mainly on Christ the Coming One, who is now central in his churches. Even though all the characteristics of the seven churches of Asia have existed from John's day to the present, certain features were especially prevalent during each of the seven major periods of church history. At least four reasons compel us to believe that we are now living in the Philadelphian age. First, the church today is undertaking the greatest missionary and evangelistic outreach in its entire history. She is truly using the "open door" of evangelism. Second, the open door of evangelism becomes the open door of the rapture in Revelation 4 and 12, for there we see the saints in heaven before the beginning of the Great Tribulation. Third, Philadelphia is the only church which is promised escape from that worldwide hour of trial, the Great Tribulation. Fourth, the second advent is never again mentioned after Philadelphia, implying that Christ has already come.

Christ is the center of worship in Revelation, beginning with the prologue and its ascription of praise based on Christ's faithfulness, resurrection, kingship, and redemption. John reacts to the appearance of Christ in Chapter 1 by worshiping prostrate at the feet of his transcendent Lord.

In Chapter 5 Christ is worshiped as the Lion of the tribe of Judah and the slain Lamb, for he is the only Person in all the universe found worthy to open the seven-sealed book. In Chapter 7 he is worshiped by the great multitude of Gentiles whom he saved and translated out of the Great Tribulation before the opening of the seventh seal. In Chapter 15 he is worshiped by a group of overcomers who have "come off victorious from the beast, and from his image, and from the number of his name" (15:2). In Chapter 19 the triune God is worshiped in four great hallelujahs by various congregations. Finally they join in an overwhelming Hallelujah Chorus of praise as every system of false worship and the entire tyranny of the Antichrist is destroyed forever.

All this holy worship contrasts sharply with the idolatrous worship of the Beast in Chapter 13 and the consequent doom of the atheist earth-dwellers to eternal punishment in the lake of fire. The whole Babylonish system of religious and political confusion which began in Genesis 10 and 11 culminates in Revelation 17 and 18, where its doom is described in full. Here both Roman Catholicism and apostate Protestantism meet their long-deserved destruction.

Then the tide of God's justice is turned by the personal return of the King of kings and Lord of lords (Revelation 19). The armies of heaven follow Christ "upon white horses, clothed in fine linen, white and pure" (19:14). In Chapters 4 and 12 Christ comes *for* his saints, but in Chapter 19 he comes *with* his saints to rule with a rod of iron (19:15). His enemies are destroyed and the Devil is bound for a thousand years in the abyss. At this time all the injustices of the past are resolved and the saints receive their eternal reward.

Then follows the great white throne judgment of the unsaved dead and their eternal consignment to the lake of fire. At the appearance of the Judge of all the earth, heaven and earth flee away to make room for the *new* heaven and *new* earth of the eternal ages.

Finally comes the New Jerusalem, the home of the bride and wife of the Lamb. It is a city so magnificent that human language only hints at its true beauty and splendor. Here we are reminded that only the *overcomer* shall inherit all these things: "And I will be his God, and he shall be my son. But for the fearful, and unbelieving, and abominable, and murderers, and fornicators, and sorcerers, and idolators, and all liars, their part shall be in the lake that burneth with fire and brimstone, which is the second death" (21:7, 8). But the invitation of the Spirit and the bride is, "Come . . . take the water of life freely" (22:17).

The apex of the Revelation is Jesus' glad promise, "I come quickly." Here stands the highest peak of emphasis in the whole Book. On this supreme promise we must concentrate all our attention. Nowhere does biblical prophecy suggest that we should look for the Antichrist, though of course today's world seems more than ready for his appearance. The only right response to the amazing news that Jesus is coming is the bursting shout of our hearts, "Amen, come Lord Jesus!"

SAMPLE PARAGRAPH CHART
OF THE REVELATION

Author: John the Apostle.
Purpose: To show Christ's slaves the things
    which must shortly come to pass (1:1).
Recipients: Seven churches of Asia.
Source: The Eternal Father, Spirit, and Son.
Theme: The personal universal coming of Christ.
Signature: The eternal, almighty Son (1:8).
Key Verses: 1:19, 20, indicating the chronological divisions.
Key Phrase: "In the Spirit" (1:10; 4:2; 17:3; 21:10). This
    indicates the Christological or biographical divisions
    and focuses the whole book on Christ.
Key Words: Sign, Signify, Wonder, Wonderful, Mystery.
Date: c. A.D. 95.
Crux: The taking of the title deed by the Slain Lamb (Ch. 5).
Climax: The Revelation of Christ (Ch. 19).

The above is a suggested beginning for your chart. Finish this chart on your own while studying Revelation. See page 30.

SAMPLE VERTICAL CHART
OF THE SEVEN CHURCHES OF ASIA
(to be completed by the student)

Division	Ref.	EPHESUS	Ref.	SMYRNA
COMMIS-SION	2:1	To the angel of the church in Ephesus write:	2:8	And to the angel of the church in Smyrna write:
DESIG-NATION	2:1	These things saith he that holdeth the seven stars in his right hand, he that walketh in the midst of the seven golden candle-sticks:	2:8	These things saith the first and the last, who was dead, and lived again:
COMMEN-DATION	2:2,3	I know thy works, and thy toil and patience, and that thou canst not bear evil men, and didst try them that call themselves apos-tles, and they are not, and didst find them false; and thou hast pa-tience and didst bear for my name's sake, and hast not grown weary.	2:9	I know thy tribu-lation and thy poverty (but thou art rich), and the blasphemy of them that say they are Jews, and they are not, but are a syna-gogue of Satan.
CONDEM-NATION	2:4	But I have this against thee, that thou didst leave thy first love.		
EXHOR-TATION	2:5	Remember there-fore whence thou art fallen, and repent and do the first works;	2:10	Fear not the things which thou art about to suffer:

Division	Ref.	EPHESUS	Ref.	SMYRNA
PRE-DICTION	2:5,6	Or else I come to thee, and will move thy candle-stick out of its place, except thou repent. But this thou hast, that thou hatest the works of the Nicolaitans, which I also hate.	2:10	Behold, the devil is about to cast some of you into prison, that ye may be tried; and ye shall have tribulation ten days. Be thou faithful unto death, and I will give thee a crown of life.
ADMO-NITION	2:7	He that hath an ear, let him hear what the Spirit saith to the churches.	2:11	He that hath an ear, let him hear what the Spirit saith to the churches.
PROMISE	2:7	To him that over-cometh will I give to eat of the tree of life, which is in the Paradise of God.	2:11	He that over-cometh shall not be hurt of the second death.

CHRONOLOGICAL RIBBON CHART OF THE REVELATION

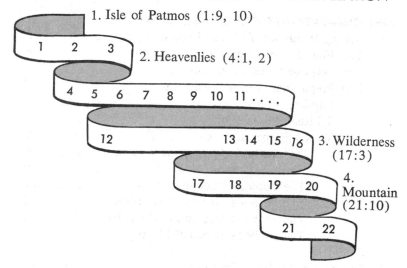

1. Isle of Patmos (1:9, 10)
2. Heavenlies (4:1, 2)
3. Wilderness (17:3)
4. Mountain (21:10)

1 2 3

4 5 6 7 8 9 10 11 ....

12 13 14 15 16

17 18 19 20

21 22

John's Prologue (1:1-8)	CHRIST CORRESPONDING
1. John's First Vision (1:9—3:22)	CHRIST IN THE CHURCHES
2. John's Second Vision (4:1—16:21)	CHRIST IN THE CONFLICT
3. John's Third Vision (17:1—20:15)	CHRIST IN THE CONQUEST
4. John's Fourth Vision (21:1—22:5)	CHRIST IN THE CONSUMMATION
John's Epilogue (22:6-21)	CHRIST CALLING

Note that Chapters 4 and 12 begin at the same point of time, and that Chapters 13, 14, 15, and 16 give further details of Chapter 11. The fall of religious Babylon announced in Chapter 14 is fully described in Chapter 17, and the fall of commercial Babylon or political Babylon announced in Chapter 16 is fully described in Chapter 18. All of these events are within the Great Tribulation period. This ribbon chart is adapted from a chart used by Harold M. Freligh.

DETAILED STUDY OUTLINE OF
A PERSONAL ADVENTURE IN PROPHECY

BIBLIOGRAPHY

The following bibliography is selective rather than exhaustive, and it is classified under three headings. The first list includes commentaries on Revelation as a whole, and the brief annotations are designed to help the student who will be reading in this field for the first time. The second list includes books on the subject of the Rapture as related to the Great Tribulation, and the third list is general. This last list includes not only books on the general subject of prophecy, but also books related to and quoted in this volume.

Revelation

Adams, John Quincy. *His Apocalypse*. Dallas: The Prophetical Society, 1924. Futurist. Selective rapture (p. 158). Woman of Rev. 12 is the church visible; man-child is the bride. The author sets dates.

Alford, Henry. The Greek Testament. Chicago: Moody Press, 1958.

Barclay, William. "The Revelation of John." In *The Daily Study Bible*. 2nd ed. Philadelphia: Westminster Press, 1960.

Barnes, Albert. *Notes on the New Testament: Revelation*. London: Blackie and Son, n.d. Year-Day principle. Historicist.

Baxter, J. Sidlow. *Explore the Book*. Vol. 6. London: Marshall, Morgan, and Scott, Ltd., 1955. Futurist and midtribulationist.

Beasley-Murray, G. R. "The Revelation." In *The New Bible Commentary*. 2nd ed. London: Inter-Varsity Fellowship, 1954.

Beckwith, Isbon T. *The Apocalypse of John*. Grand Rapids: Baker Book House, [1919], 1967.

Blaney, Harvey J. S. "Revelation." In *The Wesleyan Bible Commentary*. Vol. 6. Grand Rapids: Wm. B. Eerdmans Publishing Co., 1966.

Bloomfield, Arthur E. *All Things New—A Study of Revelation*. Minneapolis: Bethany Fellowship, Inc., 1959.

Bowman, John Wick. *The Drama of the Book of Revelation*. Philadelphia: Westminster Press, 1955.

Brodie, Frederick. *The Revelation*. London: Partridge and Co., 1881. Synchronous group; no chronological order. Contains a chart of explanation of different numbers of days of Daniel, referring to the Tribulation.

Carpenter, W. Boyd. *Ellicott's Commentary on the Whole Bible*. Vol. 8. Grand Rapids: Zondervan Publishing House, n.d. Symbolical group.

Caird, G. B. *A Commentary on the Revelation of St. John the Divine*. New York and Evanston: Harper and Row, 1960.

Charles, R. H. "The Revelation of St. John." In *The International Critical Commentary*. Vol. 1. Edinburgh: T. & T. Clark, 1920.

Critical treatment of text. Liberal. Synchronous group. Not purely symbolical; Millennium taken literally. Author uses the philological method; believes St. John used sources.

Clarke, Adam. "The Revelation of St. John the Divine." In *The New Testament of Our Lord and Saviour Jesus Christ with a Commentary and Critical Notes.* Vol. 2. New York: Carlton and Phillips, 1854. Takes no particular viewpoint; says he does not understand the Book.

Earle, Ralph. "The Book of Revelation." In *Beacon Bible Commentary.* Vol. 10. Kansas City, MO: Beacon Hill Press of Kansas City, 1967.

Erdman, Charles R. *The Revelation of John.* Philadelphia: Westminster Press, 1936.

Gaebelein, Arno C. *The Revelation.* New York: Loizeaux Brothers, Inc., 1961. Futurist. Premillennial and dispensational.

Glasson, T. F. "The Revelation of John." In *The Cambridge Bible Commentary.* Cambridge: University Press, 1965.

Godbey, W. B. "Revelation." In *Commentary on the New Testament.* Vol. 1. Cincinnati: Revivalist Office, 1896.

Gordon, S. D. *Quiet Talks about Our Lord's Return.* New York: Fleming H. Revell Co., 1912. Synchronous group. Rev. 6-18 regarded as seven different views of the same run of events, taking place in 3½ years (p. 123). Week-Year theory of Daniel's 70 weeks. Premillennial; posttribulational (pp. 75, 109, 143).

Harrison, Norman B. *Re-Thinking the Revelation.* Minneapolis: The Harrison Service, 1941. Futurist. The Great Tribulation begins at Rev. 12 rather than Rev. 6, and the Church is translated at the blowing of the seventh trumpet of Rev. 11; this is called the "last" trumpet and identified with 1 Cor. 15:51, 52.

Hendricksen, W. *More Than Conquerors—An Interpretation of the Book of Revelation.* 5th ed. Grand Rapids: Baker Book House, 1949.

Henry, Matthew. *Matthew Henry's Commentary on the Whole Bible.* Vol. 6. New York: Fleming H. Revell, n.d. Historicist.

Heslop, William G. *Riches from Revelation.* Butler, IN: The Higley Press, 1932. Futurist.

Ironside, Harry Allan. *Lectures on the Book of Revelation.* Neptune, NJ: Loizeaux Brothers, 1953.

Jamieson, Robert, Fausset, A. R., and Brown, David. "The Revelation of St. John the Divine." In *A Commentary on the Old and New Testaments.* Vol. 6. Grand Rapids: Wm. B. Eerdmans Publishing Co., 1945. Historicist. Believes in the threefold division suggested in 1:19, but sees the seals, trumpets, and vials as parallel.

Kiddle, Martin. "The Revelation of St. John." In *Moffatt New Testament Commentary.* New York: Harper and Brothers, n.d.

Kuyper, Abraham. *The Revelation of St. John.* Grand Rapids: Wm. B. Eerdmans Publishing Co., [1935], 1963.

Lange, John Peter. "Revelation." In *Commentary on the Holy Scriptures.* Vol. 24. Grand Rapids: Zondervan Publishing House, n.d. Presents various viewpoints.

Larkin, Clarence. *The Book of Revelation.* Philadelphia: Rev. Clarence

Larkin Estate, 1919. Futurist; dispensation; premillennial; pretribulational.

Laymon, Charles M. *The Book of Revelation.* New York and Nashville: Abingdon Press, 1960. Preterist and idealist. Includes a chart from *Interpreter's Bible.*

Lenski, Richard Charles Henry. *Interpretation of St. John's Revelation.* Minneapolis: Augsburg Publishing House [1943], 1961. Synchronous group; amillennial; nondispensational. The visions present lines or vistas—not chronological. These start at various points but all focus upon the final judgment and eternal triumph.

Love, Julian Price. "The Revelation to John." In *The Layman's Bible Commentary.* Vol. 25. Richmond, VA: John Knox Press, 1960.

McDowell, Edward A. *The Meaning and Message of the Book of Revelation.* Nashville: Broadman Press, 1951. Preterist.

Moffatt, James. "The Revelation of St. John the Divine." In *Expositor's Greek Testament.* Vol. 5. New York and London: Hodder and Stoughton, n.d.

Morgan, G. Campbell. *The Letters of Our Lord.* London: Pickering and Inglis, [1945], 1956.

Newell, William R. *The Book of Revelation.* Chicago: Moody Press, 1935. Futurist; dispensational. The woman of Rev. 12 is Israel.

Newberry, Thomas. *Notes on the Revelation.* Kilmarnock, Scotland: John Ritchie, Pub., 1840. Futurist. Woman in Rev. 12 is Israel under the new covenant. Man-child is the believing portion of Israel during the times of Antichrist divided into three companies.

Ottman, Ford C. *The Unfolding of the Ages in the Revelation of John.* New York: The Baker and Taylor Co., 1905. Futurist; premillennial. Woman is Israel; man-child is Christ.

Parker, Joseph. "Ephesians to Revelation." In *The People's Bible.* Vol. 27. New York and London: Funk and Wagnalls Co., n.d.

Plummer, A. "Revelation." In *The Pulpit Commentary.* Vol. 51. Chicago: Wilcox and Follett Co., n.d. Letters to the churches are historical and typical—not pictures of successive ages of church history. Twenty-four elders are churches of the Old and New Testaments. Seals, trumpets, and vials run parallel.

Ramsey, William. *Letters to the Seven Churches of Asia and Their Place in the Plan of the Apocalypse.* Grand Rapids: Baker Book House, 1963 reprint. Preterist. Best for historical background.

Richardson, Donald W. *The Revelation of Jesus Christ.* Richmond, VA: John Knox Press, 1964.

Rist, Martin. "The Revelation." In *The Interpreter's Bible.* Vol. 12. New York: Abingdon Press, 1957.

Roadhouse, William Frederick. *Seeing the "Revelation."* Toronto: The Overcomer Publishers, 1932. Synchronous group. All sections of Revelation are regarded concurrent, contemporaneous, and coterminous. Dispensational; midtribulational. Threefold division of Rev. 1:19 rejected.

Sale-Harrison, L. *The Wonders of the Great Unveiling—The Remark-*

able Book of the Revelation. London: Pickering and Inglis Ltd., n.d.

Scott, C. Anderson. *The Book of Revelation.* New York: Hodder and Stoughton, n.d. Historicist (pp. 174ff).

Scott, Walter. *Exposition of the Revelation of Jesus Christ.* London: Pickering and Inglis, Ltd., n.d.

Scroggie, W. Graham. *The Great Unveiling—The Book of the Revelation.* London: Oliphants, Ltd., n.d.

Seiss, Joseph Augustus. *The Apocalypse.* Grand Rapids: Zondervan Publishing House, n.d. Futurist. One of the first premillennial, futurist commentaries on Revelation to become popular; extremely influential. The author supports the selective rapture theory.

—————. *Letters to the Seven Churches.* Grand Rapids: Baker Book House, 1956 reprint.

Simpson, Albert Benjamin. *The Coming One.* New York: Christian Alliance Publishing Co., 1912. Historicist; premillennial; selective rapture theory; Year-Day theory.

Smith, J. B. *A Revelation of Jesus Christ.* Scottdale, PA: Herald Press, 1961. Futurist; premillennial; pretribulational (p. 333).

Stearns, D. M. *Studies in the Book of Revelation.* Harrisburg: Fred Kelker, 1923. Futurist.

Strauss, Lehman. *The Book of Revelation.* Neptune, NJ: Loizeaux Brothers, 1964.

Swete, Henry Barclay. *The Apocalypse of St. John.* Grand Rapids: Wm. B. Eerdmans Publishing Co., 1954. Reprint from 1908. Does not identify himself with any one school of interpretation. Explains the first five seals by contemporary historical method. Regards the messages to the seven churches as not directly prophetical. Believes in the inspiration and essential unity of the book. No express predictions of persons and actions. No exact chronological order, but general prophecies similar to Old Testament. Amillennial.

Tait, Andrew. *The Messages to the Seven Churches of Asia Minor.* London: Hodder and Stoughton, 1884.

Tenney, Merrill C. *Interpreting Revelation.* Grand Rapids: Wm. B. Eerdmans Publishing Co., 1957. Premillennial; moderate futurist group.

Thompson, J. L. *That Glorious Future!* London: Logan Thompson, n.d. Futurist; pretribulational; partial rapture. Woman is the visible church; man-child is the overcomers.

Torrance, Thomas F. *The Apocalypse Today.* Grand Rapids: Wm. B. Eerdmans Publishing Co., 1959. Historicist; amillennial (p. 136). Woman is Israel; man-child is Christ. Rev. 19 is the earthly church entering into her heavenly state. The rider on the white horse in Rev. 6 is Antichrist.

Tuck, Robert. "The Revelation of St. John the Divine." In *The Preacher's Complete Homiletical Commentary.* New York: Funk and Wagnalls, 1896. Historicist.

Walvoord, John F. *The Revelation of Jesus Christ.* Chicago: Moody Press, 1966. Premillennial; dispensational; pretribulational.

Wesley, John. *Explanatory Notes upon the New Testament.* London: Epworth Press, 1941. Reprint.

Williams, Isaac. *The Apocalypse.* London: Francis and John Rivington, 1852. Symbolical group (p. 308).

Rapture

Amerding, Carl. "That Blessed Hope." In *Bibliotheca Sacra* (April, 1954), 149-157.

Bradbury, John W. ed. *Hastening the Day of God.* Wheaton: Van Kampen Press, 1953. Prophetic messages from the International Congress on Prophecy in Calvary Baptist Church, New York City, November 9-16, 1952. Pretribulational.

_____. *The Sure Word of Prophecy.* New York: Fleming H. Revell Company, 1943. Report of the New York Congress on Prophecy assembled in the Calvary Baptist Church, New York City, November 1-8, 1942.

Cuthbertson, William, and Centz, Herman B., editors. *Understanding the Times.* Travelers Rest, South Carolina: Southern Bible Book House, 1954. Prophetic messages delivered at the Second International Congress on Prophecy, New York City. Pretribulational.

David, Ira E. "Translation: When Does It Occur?" *The Alliance Weekly* (March 30, 1935), pp. 196-197.

English, E. Schuyler. *Re-Thinking the Rapture.* Travelers Rest, South Carolina: Southern Bible Book House, 1954. An examination of what the Scriptures teach as to the time of the translation of the church in relation to the tribulation. Pretribulational.

Hamilton, Gavin. *The Rapture and the Great Tribulation.* New York: Loizeaux Brothers, 1957. Pretribulational.

Harris, John A. *The Second Coming of Our Lord Jesus Christ in Relation to Israel, the Church, and the World.* Stretford, Manchester: the Author, n.d. Selective rapture.

Harrison, William K. "The Time of the Rapture as Indicated in Certain Scriptures." In *Bibliotheca Sacra.* October, 1957 to July, 1958. Pretribulational.

Kopecky, Donald W. "Salvation in the Tribulation." In *Bibliotheca Sacra* (July—December, 1952). Pretribulational.

Ladd, George Eldon. *The Blessed Hope.* Grand Rapids: Zondervan Publishing House, 1956. Posttribulational; non-dispensational.

Lang, G. H. *Firstfruits and Harvest—A Study in Resurrection and Rapture.* 2nd ed. Wimborne, Dorset: Of the Author, 1946. Two-rapture view: one before the Great Tribulation and one afterwards. Two-resurrection view: one after the Great Tribulation of saints only, and one after the millennium of saints and sinners.

Ludwigson, R. *Bible Prophecy Notes.* Grand Rapids: Zondervan Publishing House, 1956. A good presentation of all three millennial and and tribulational viewpoints.

Marsh, F. E. *What Will Take Place When Christ Returns?* London and Glasgow: Pickering and Inglis, n.d. Pretribulational; premillennial. Pre-Resurrection of the church before the Tribulation (1 Cor. 15:23; 1 Thess. 4). First resurrection of tribulation saints after the Tribulation (Rev. 20:4-6). Second resurrection, of wicked dead, after the Millennium.

Ockenga, Harold John, and Walvoord, John. "Will the Church Go through the Tribulation?" In *Christian Life* (February, 1955). A presentation of both posttribulational and pretribulational viewpoints.

Panton, D. M. *Rapture*. London: Chas. J. Thynne, 1922. Selective rapture.

Payne, J. Barton. *The Imminent Appearing of Christ*. Grand Rapids: Wm. B. Eerdmans Publishing Company, 1962. Posttribulational. An effort to reconcile the doctrine of imminency with the classical posttribulational viewpoint.

Simpson, Albert Benjamin. *Days of Heaven upon Earth*. Harrisburg, Pennsylvania: Christian Publications, Incorporated, 1925. Selective rapture, p. 76.

————. *Romans*. Harrisburg, Pennsylvania: Christian Publications, Inc., n.d. Selective rapture (pp. 182-183).

Stanton, Gerald B. *Kept from the Hour*. Grand Rapids: Zondervan Publishing House, 1956. Pretribulational.

Strombeck, J. F. *First the Rapture*. Wheaton: Van Kampen Press, 1951. Pretribulational.

Tenney, Merrill C. "Eschatology and the Pulpit." In *Bibliotheca Sacra* (January, 1959). Does not set forth any special theory, but heartily recommends preaching on eschatology.

Thiessen, Henry Clarence. *Will the Church Pass through the Tribulation?* New York: Loizeaux Brothers, Publishers, 1941. Pretribulational.

Walvoord, John F. "Dispensational Premillennialism." In *Christianity Today*. September 15, 1958.

————. *The Rapture Question*. Findlay, Ohio: Dunham Publishing Company, 1957. Pretribulational.

————. *The Return of the Lord*. Findlay, Ohio: Dunham Publishing Company, 1955. Pretribulational.

Wuest, Kenneth S. "The Rapture—Precisely When?" In *Bibliotheca Sacra* (January, 1957). Pretribulational.

Whiting, Arthur B. "The Rapture of the Church." In *Bibliotheca Sacra* (July—December, 1945). Pretribulational.

Wood, Leon J. *Is the Rapture Next?* Grand Rapids: Zondervan Publishing House, 1956. Pretribulational. *Apostasía* in 2 Thess. 2 is said to mean "rapture."

General

Amerding, Carl. "Will There Be Another Elijah?" In *Bibliotheca Sacra* (January—March, 1943).

Arndt, William F. and Gingrich, F. Wilbur. *A Greek-English Lexicon of the New Testament.* Chicago: The University of Chicago Press, 1957.

Bauman, Louis S. *Light from Bible Prophecy.* New York: Fleming H. Revell Company, 1960. Pretribulational. Discusses Dan. 2 and Ezek. 38, 39.

Blackstone, W. E. *Jesus Is Coming.* New York: Fleming H. Revell Company, 1908. Pretribulational. Has been translated into 36 foreign languages. The author was one of the early official workers in The Christian and Missionary Alliance.

Bradbury, John W., ed. *The Sure Word of Prophecy.* New York: Fleming H. Revell Company, 1943. Pretribulational.

_____. *Hastening the Day of God.* Wheaton: Van Kampen Press, 1952.

Cuthbertson, William, and Centz, Herman B. *Understanding the Times.* Grand Rapids: Zondervan Publishing House, 1956.

Deissman, Adolf. *Light from the Ancient East.* 4th rev. ed. Grand Rapids: Baker Book House, 1965.

Drummond, Roscoe. "United States of Europe—Hope of the West." In *The Reader's Digest* (February, 1962).

Encyclopedia Britannica. 14th ed. Vol. 16. "Numerals."

Evans, W. Glyn. "Will Babylon Be Restored?" In *Bibliotheca Sacra* (July—December, 1950).

Free, Joseph P. *Archaeology and Bible History.* Wheaton: Van Kampen Press, 1950.

Gaebelein, Arno C. *As It Was—So Shall It Be—A Study of the First Age and Our Present Age.* New York: Publication Office of *Our Hope,* 1937. Pretribulational.

_____. *Christ and Glory.* New York: Publication Office of *Our Hope,* 1918.

_____. *The Conflict of the Ages—The Mystery of Lawlessness: Its Origin, Historic Development and Coming Defeat.* New York: Publication Office of *Our Hope,* 1933.

_____. *The Harmony of the Prophetic Word.* New York: Publication Office of *Our Hope,* 1907.

Graham, Billy. "Facing the Anti-God Colossus." In *Christianity Today* (December 21, 1962).

Gray, James M. *Synthetic Bible Studies.* New York: Fleming H. Revell Company, 1923.

Haldeman, I. M. *The Coming of Christ Both Premillennial and Imminent.* Philadelphia: Philadelphia School of the Bible, 1906.

Hamilton, Floyd E. *The Basis of the Christian Faith.* Rev. and enl. ed. New York, Evanston, and London: Harper and Row, 1964.

Harrison, William K. "As Ye See the Day Approaching." In *Bibliotheca Sacra* (January, 1959).

Henry, Carl F. H. "Diversity in Unity: Report on New Delhi." In *Christianity Today* (December 22, 1961).

Heslop, W. G. *The Coming Collapse.* Butler, Indiana: The Higley Press, 1937.

James, E. O. *The Cult of the Mother-Goddess.* London: Thames and Hudson, 1959.

Kittel, Gerard ed. *Theological Dictionary of the New Testament.* Grand Rapids: Wm. B. Eerdmans Publishing Company, 1964-.

Langston, E. L. *How God Is Working to a Plan.* London and Edinburgh: Marshall, Morgan and Scott, Limited, n.d.

Larkin, Clarence. *Dispensational Truth.* Philadelphia. Rev. Clarence Larkin Estate, 1920. Pretribulational.

Liddell, Henry George, and Scott, Robert. *A Greek-English Lexicon.* Oxford: At the Clarendon Press, [1843], 1953.

Morgan, G. Campbell. *God's Method with Men.* New York: Fleming H. Revell Company, 1898. Selective rapture (p. 13).

Mullett, Mary B. "How to Keep Young Mentally." In *The Reader's Digest* (February, 1922). Also see the February, 1962 issue, pp. 27-29.

Nash, Charles A. "The Scriptural View of Church History." In *Bibliotheca Sacra* (January—March, 1943).

Otto, Rudolph. *The Idea of the Holy.* London, New York, Toronto: Oxford University Press, 1950.

Pache, René. *The Return of Jesus Christ.* Translated by William Sanford LaSor. Chicago: Moody Press, 1955.

Panin, Ivan. *Bible Numerics.* Vancouver, British Columbia: The British Israel Association, n.d. During his lifetime, the author had no connection with The British Israel Association, but in view of the fact that his words are no longer available, permission to reprint was granted by Mr. C. M. Ambridge, Trustee for the Works of Ivan Panin in America.

_____. *The Shorter Works of Ivan Panin.* Vancouver, British Columbia: The British Israel Association, n.d.

Pankhurst, Christabel. *The World's Unrest: Vision of the Dawn.* Philadelphia: The Sunday School Times Company, n.d.

Parliman, Mrs. J. Austin. "The Sleep of Muiri." *The Alliance Witness* (December 31, 1958). Modern illustrations of the Beast of Rev. 13.

Pember, G. H. *The Great Prophecies Concerning the Gentiles, the Jews, and the Church of God.* London: Hodder and Stoughton, 1881.

Pentecost, J. Dwight. "The Godly Remnant of the Tribulation Period." In *Bibliotheca Sacra* (April, 1960).

_____. *Prophecy for Today.* Grand Rapids: Zondervan Publishing House, 1961.

Peters, George N. H. *The Theocratic Kingdom.* 3 vol. Grand Rapids: Kregel Publications, 1957. Premillennial; selective rapture.

Petrie, Arthur. *Behind the Berlin Crisis and the Signs of the End.* Seattle, Washington: Arthur Petrie, n.d.

Philadelphia Prophetic Conference. *Light on Prophecy.* New York: The Christian Bible House, 1918. Pretribulational.

Phillipps, O. E. *Birth Pangs of a New Age.* Philadelphia: Hebrew Christian Fellowship, Inc., 1955. Pretribulational.

Rimmer, Harry. *Straight Ahead Lies Yesterday.* Grand Rapids: Wm. B. Eerdmans Publishing Company, 1945.

Robertson, Archibald Thomas. "The General Epistles and the Apocalypse." In *Word Pictures in the New Testament.* Vol. 6. Nashville: Broadman Press, 1931.

Rogers, W. H. *"The End from the Beginning"—A Panorama of Prophecy or History, the Mould of Prediction.* New York: Arno C. Gaebelein, Inc., 1938. Pretribulational. A good comprehensive view of the whole subject of prophecy and a good study of Dan. 9:24-27.

Sandegren, C. "The Addressees of the Epistle to the Hebrews." In *The Evangelical Quarterly* (October, 1955).

Scofield, C. I. *What Do the Prophets Say?* Philadelphia: The Sunday School Times Company, 1916.

Smith, Oswald J. *The Clouds Are Lifting.* London and Edinburgh: Marshall, Morgan & Scott, Limited, 1939.

_____. *The Dawn Is Breaking.* London and Edinburgh: Marshall, Morgan & Scott, Limited, n.d.

_____. *Prophecy—What Lies Ahead?* London and Edinburgh: Marshall, Morgan & Scott, Limited, 1952.

_____. *The Voice of Prophecy.* London and Edinburgh: Marshall, Morgan & Scott, Limited, 1950.

_____. *World Problems in the Light of Prophecy.* London and Edinburgh: Marshall, Morgan & Scott, Limited, n.d.

Smith, Wilbur. *World Crises and the Prophetic Scriptures.* Chicago: Moody Press, 1950.

Springer, J. A. *Outlines on Prophecy.* Cleveland: Light and Hope Publishing Company, 1903.

Sumrall, Lester F. *Roman Catholicism Slays.* Grand Rapids: Zondervan Publishing House, 1940.

Thayer, Joseph Henry. *Greek-English Lexicon of the New Testament.* New York: American Book Co., 1889.

Thiessen, Henry Clarence. *Introduction to the New Testament.* Grand Rapids: Wm. B. Eerdmans Publishing Co., 1950.

Time—The Weekly News Magazine. "Pope John XXIII, Man of the Year" (January 4, 1963).

Traina, Robert A. *Methodical Bible Study.* New York: The Biblical Seminary, 1952.

Trench, Richard Chenevix. *Synonyms of the New Testament.* Grand Rapids: Wm. B. Eerdmans Publishing Co., 1880, 1960.

Unger, Merrill F. *Great Neglected Bible Prophecies.* Chicago: Scripture Press Book Division, 1955. Ezek. 37; Ezekiel's Temple; Paul's Judgment Seat of Christ; Paul's Olive Tree and Israel's Future.

Vincent, Marvin R. *Word Studies in the New Testament.* Vol. 2. Grand Rapids: Wm. B. Eerdmans Publishing Co., 1946.

Vos, Geerhardus. *The Pauline Eschatology.* Grand Rapids: Wm. B. Eerdmans Publishing Co., 1953. Amillennial.

Wells, Robert J., ed. *Prophetic Messages for Modern Times.* Dallas: Texas Printing House, Inc., 1944.

Wyngaarden, Martin J. *The Future of the Kingdom in Prophecy and Fulfillment.* Grand Rapids: Baker Book House, 1955. Amillennial.